JOURNEYS

Practice Book

Volume 2

Grade 1

HOUGHTON MIFFLIN HARCOURT
School Publishers

Printed in the U.S.A.

ISBN 10: 0-54-724910-1
ISBN 13: 978-0-54-724910-0

11 0868 17 16 15 14 13 12

4500377232

Contents

Name ___________________________________

Words to Know

Listen to the clues and read along.
Circle the best answer to each clue.

1. This means **in a circle.**	**around**	**think**
2. This means **not heavy.**	**because**	**light**
3. You do this to let people look at something.	**bring**	**show**
4. After is its opposite.	**before**	**carry**
5. You do this with bags.	**carry**	**because**
6. This tells why.	**because**	**around**
7. Take away is its opposite.	**light**	**bring**
8. Your brain does this.	**think**	**before**

Name ______________________

Words with Long *o*

Read the word. Circle the picture that matches the word.

1. home

2. go

3. stone

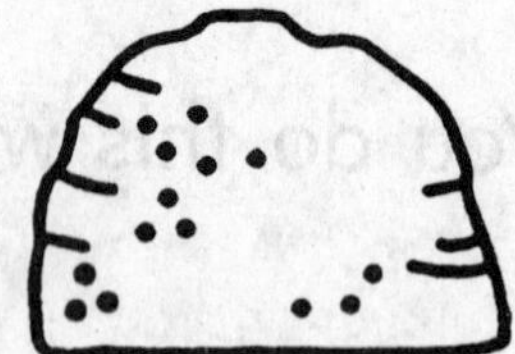

4. robe

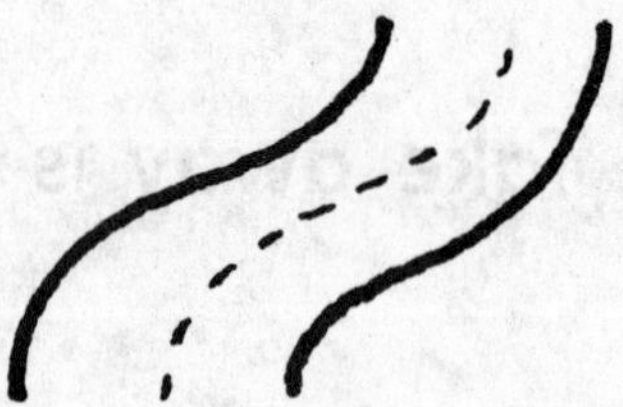

5. hole

Name ______________________________

Let's Go to the Moon!
Phonics: Words with Long *o*

Words with Long *o*

Look at the picture. Name each picture.
Write the missing letters to complete the word.

1.
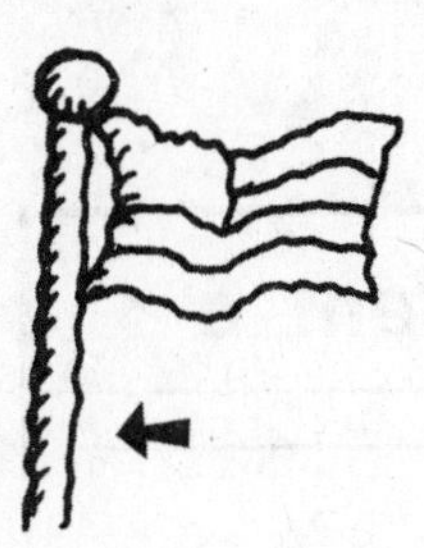

p ___ l ___

2.
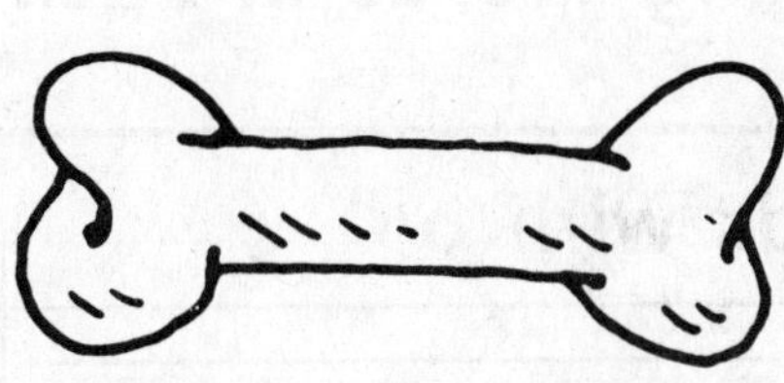

b ___ n ___

3.

g ___

4.

r ___ p ___

5.

s t ___ v ___

6.
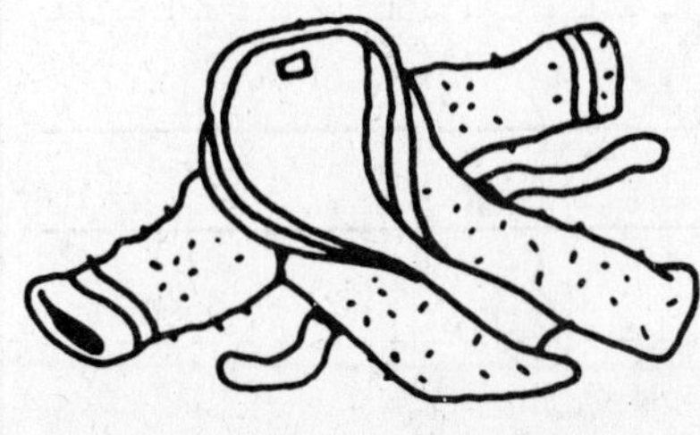

r ___ b ___

Name ______________________

Spelling Words with the Long *o* Sound

Sort the words. Write the correct Spelling Words in each column.

Ends with o	Ends with Silent e

Spelling Words

so
go
home
hole
no
rope
joke
bone
stove
poke

Name ____________________

What Is a Question?

Circle each question.

1. What did you see?

2. Can you look up?

3. Is that the sun?

4. I think I will read.

5. Where did Mike go?

6. They are at the game.

7. How many rocks does Liz have?

8. I like to tell jokes.

Name ____________________

Let's Go to the Moon!
Writing: Write to Narrate

Using Details

Draw a picture of something you discovered, or found.

Write sentences about when you saw your discovery.

One day I **found** a ____________________.

When I **saw** it, I ____________________.

Then I ____________________.

Main Idea

All my sentences tell about ____________________.

Name ___

Words with Long *u*

Circle the word that names the picture.

1. 

flute flat

2. 

mole mule

3. 

hang huge

4. 

cute cut

5. 

cone cube

Name ______________________________

Main Idea and Details

Use the web map to show the supporting details about the Moon's surface.

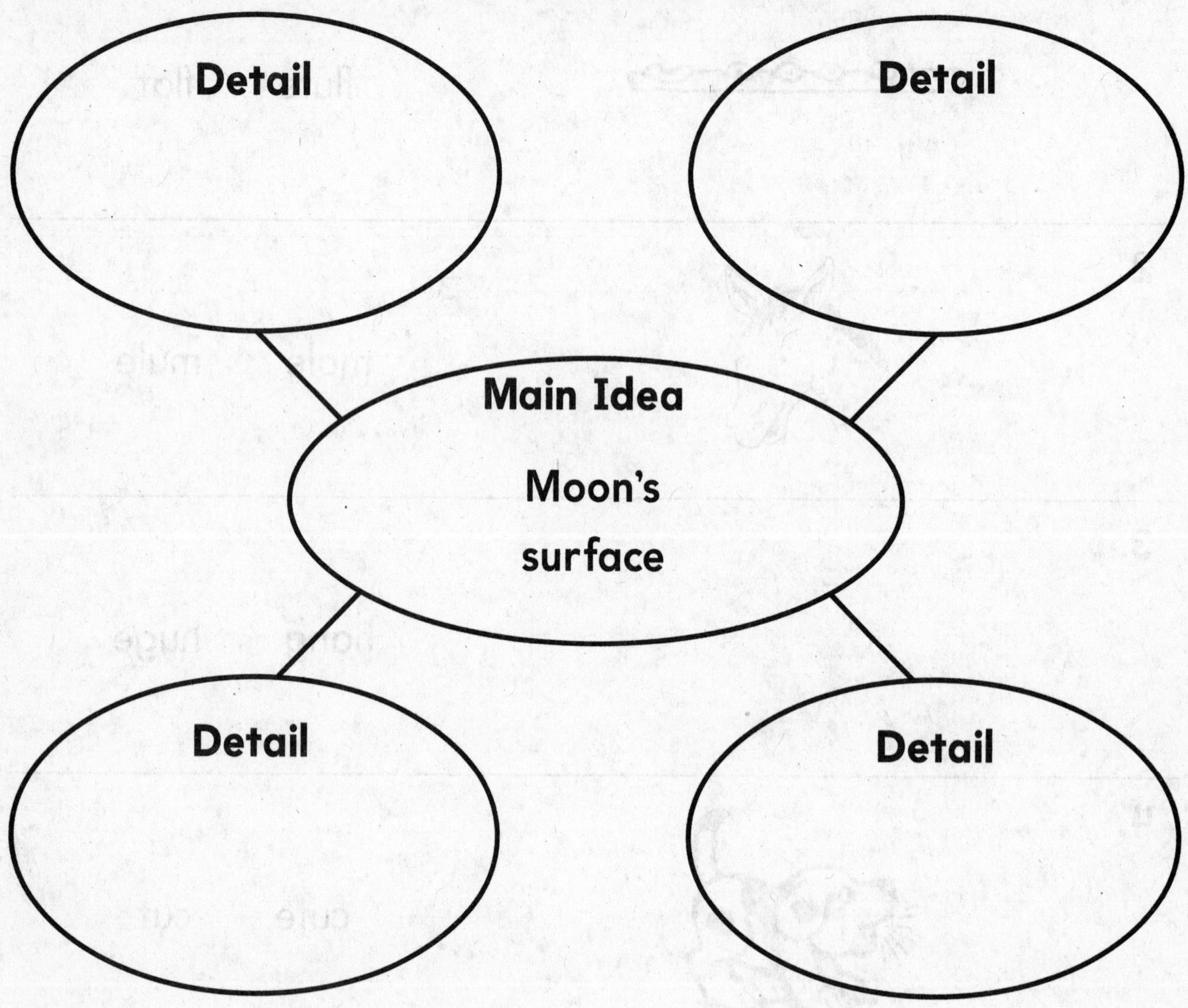

Name ______________________________

Spelling Words with the Long *o* Sound

Spelling Words

- so
- go
- home
- hole
- no
- rope
- joke
- bone
- stove
- poke

Write the Spelling Words that rhyme with woke.

1. ______________ 2. ______________

Write the Spelling Words that begin with h.

3. ______________ 4. ______________

Write the Spelling Words that rhyme with Jo.

5. ______________

6. ______________

7. ______________

Writing Questions

Write the correct word from the Word Bank to begin each sentence. Write the correct end mark.

Word Bank

What Can When Where Do Are

1. ______________ can I put my hat ____

2. ______________ can they see ____

3. ______________ you see me ____

4. ______________ you need a snack ____

5. ______________ you cold ____

6. ______________ do you go ____

Name ____________________

Let's Go to the Moon!
Writing: Write to Narrate

Planning My Sentences

Draw and write details that tell what happened.

My Topic: ____________________

First Detail

Second Detail

Third Detail

Spelling Words with the Long *o* Sound

Write a Spelling Word to complete each sentence.

Spelling Words

- so
- go
- home
- hole
- no
- rope
- joke
- bone
- stove
- poke

1. The pot on the ____________________ is hot.

2. Can you wrap the ____________________ around the pole?

3. What ____________________ does a fox live in?

4. I can tell a funny ____________________ .

5. Stand up ____________________ that I can see you.

6. It is time to ____________________ to bed.

Name ____________________

Spiral Review

Circle each proper noun. Then write the proper noun correctly.

1. My friend mel has a box of gem stones. ____________________

2. She will let kim look at it. ____________________

3. She has a dog named red. ____________________

Draw a line under each title. Then write the titles and names correctly.

4. Mom's friend is mrs. Dell. ____________________

5. Will dr. Wade visit the class? ____________________

6. I wrote to mr. Kline. ____________________

Name ______________________________

Grammar in Writing

A sentence that asks something is called a **question.** A question begins with a capital letter and ends with a **question mark.**

Fix the mistakes in these sentences. Use proofreading marks.

Examples: does the moon have plants ^?

Is the moon dusty. ^?

1. Did you know his name
2. when did they go?
3. Why do you have your bike.
4. what do cats eat?
5. is the Moon hot or cold.

Proofreading Marks	
^	Add
≡	Capital letter

Name ______________________________

Words to Know

Listen to the questions. Read along.
Circle the best answer to each question.

1. What word goes with **might**?	**maybe**	**there**
2. What word goes with **do not**?	**car**	**don't**
3. What word goes with **true**?	**could**	**sure**
4. What word goes with **drive**?	**car**	**there**
5. What word goes with **here**?	**there**	**don't**
6. What word goes with **can**?	**cart**	**could**
7. What word comes after the words **"This story is ______"**?	**don't**	**about**
8. What word tells how you travel?	**by**	**maybe**

Name ______________________

Words with Long *e*

Circle the word that matches the picture.

1.

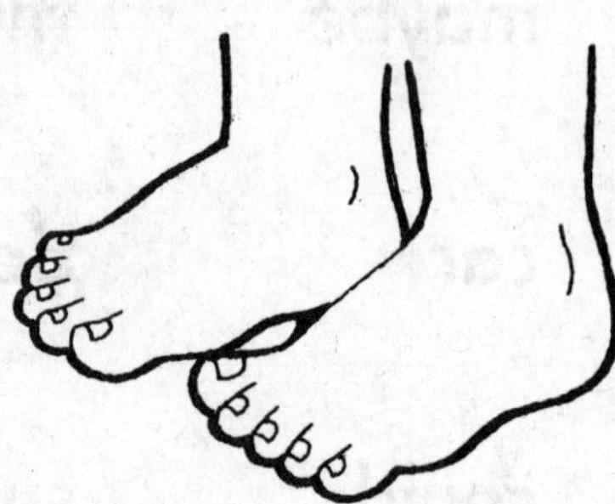

feel feet

2.

tree tea

3.

me he

4.

leaf leap

5.

seat street

6.

see bee

Name ______________________________

Words with Long e

Circle the word that completes the sentence.

1. I can ______ you how to plant seeds.

teach **beach**

2. These are big ______ .

bees **seeds**

3. I will put them in ______ holes.

jeep **deep**

4. Help me ______ my watering can.

reach **peach**

5. Before long, we will see a small ______ .

beef **leaf**

Name ______________________________

Spelling Words with the Long *e* Sound

Sort the words. Write the correct Spelling Words in each column.

Words with e	Words with ea	Words with ee

Word with Silent e

Spelling Words

me
be
read
feet
tree
keep
eat
mean
sea
these

Name ____

The Big Trip
Grammar: Kinds of Sentences

Question or Statement?

 **Draw a line under the correct sentence in each pair.**

1. Where are we going.	Where are we going?
2. A boat is fun.	A boat is fun?
3. When will we go.	When will we go?
4. Where is your bike.	Where is your bike?
5. Planes are fast.	Planes are fast?

 **Write the correct end mark to finish each sentence.**

6. Can we go out to play ____

7. Tim lost his map ____

8. Will your friend come ____

Name ________________

Details for Where and When

Draw a picture of something you saw or did on a trip.

Write sentences about your trip.

Who	Action	Where

Who	Action	When

Who	Action	Where

Name ______________________________

The Big Trip
Phonics: Words Ending with *ng, nk*

Words Ending with *ng, nk*

Circle the letters that finish the word.

Write the word.

1.

ba____

(nk, ng)

____

2.

dri____

(nk, ng)

____

3.

swi____

(nk, ng)

____

4.

ki____

(nk, ng)

____

Name ____________________

Compare and Contrast

Use the Venn diagram to tell how Pig's ideas and Goat's ideas are alike and different.

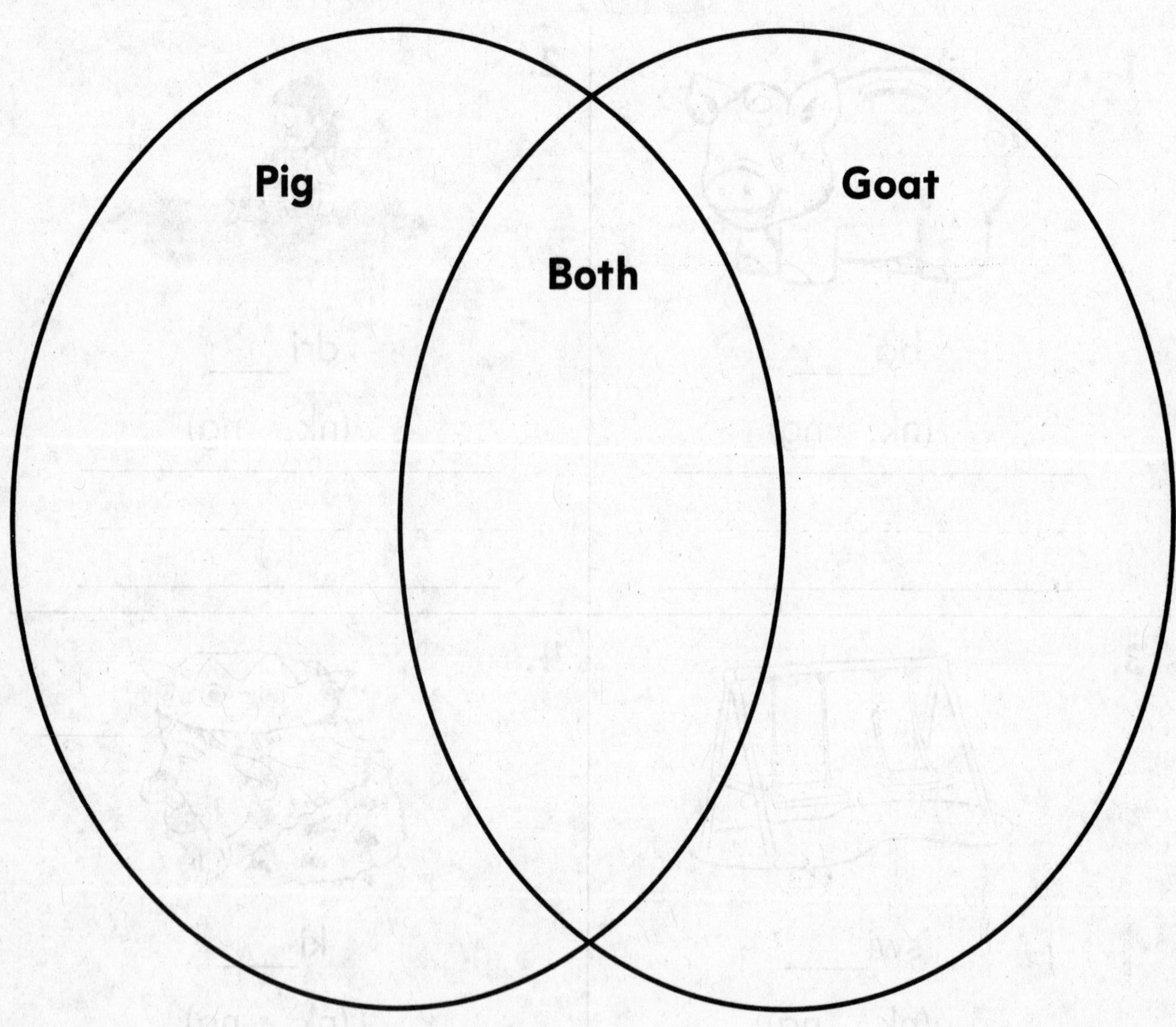

Name ______________________________

Spelling Words with the Long *e* Sound

Write the Spelling Word that names each picture.

Spelling Words

- me
- be
- read
- feet
- tree
- keep
- eat
- mean
- sea
- these

1. ______________

2. ______________

3. ______________

4. ______________

5. ______________

6. ______________

Name ______________________

Writing Questions and Statements

Decide if each sentence is a question or a statement. Then write it correctly.

1. the train is full

2. where is Mom

3. she is sitting

4. this is a long trip

5. are we there yet

Name ______________________________

Planning My Sentences

Draw and write details that tell what happened first and next.

My Topic: ______________________________

First

Next

Name ______________________________

Spelling Words with the Long *e* Sound

Write a Spelling Word from the box to complete each sentence.

Spelling Words

- me
- be
- read
- feet
- tree
- keep
- eat
- mean
- sea
- these

1. Look at the leaves on that ____________.

2. What do you ____________ in your backpack?

3. I like to swim in the ____________.

4. Pick from ____________ games.

5. A duck has two ____________.

6. Will you ____________ to me?

Name ______________________

Spiral Review

 **Circle each proper noun. Then write the proper noun correctly.**

1. I go to spring school. ______________

2. It is on pine street. ______________

 **Write each sentence correctly.**

3. They fish on moss creek.

____

4. She is going to japan.

____

Name ______________________________

Grammar in Writing

A **statement** is a telling sentence.

A **question** is an asking sentence.

Write two statements and two questions about the picture. Be sure you begin and end each sentence correctly.

Statement

____

Statement

____

Question

____

Question

____

____

Name ______________________________

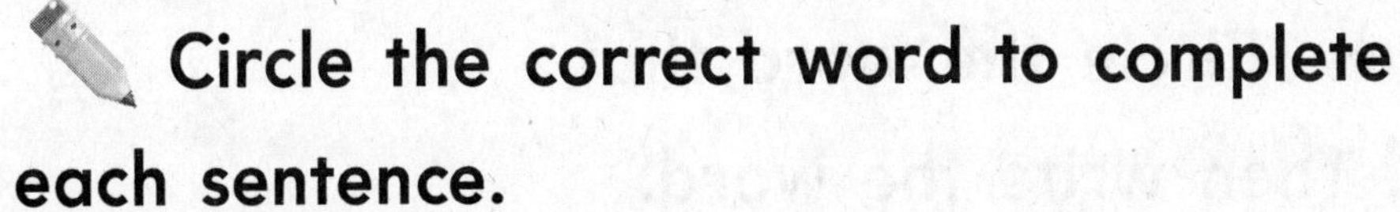

Words to Know

Circle the correct word to complete each sentence.

1. Fran ate her beets (these, first).

2. Beets are planted in the (ground, sometimes).

3. (Food, Sometimes) Fran eats salad, too.

4. Fran has to eat all the (food, your) on her plate.

5. "Eat (ground, your) peas," said Mom.

6. The peas are (your, right) from the shop.

7. Fran looked (under, first) her peas.

8. Fran said, "(These, Under) peas look good!"

Name ______________________________

Words with *ai*, *ay*

Read the words. Circle the word that names the picture. Then write the word.

1. 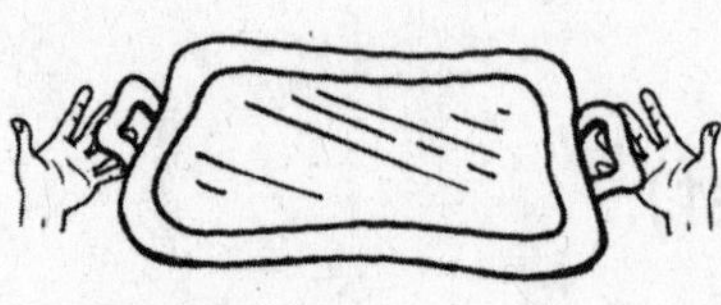

tray ray

2. 

sail nail

3. 

hay day

4. 

paint pain

5. 

train rain

Name ______________________________

Words with *ai, ay*

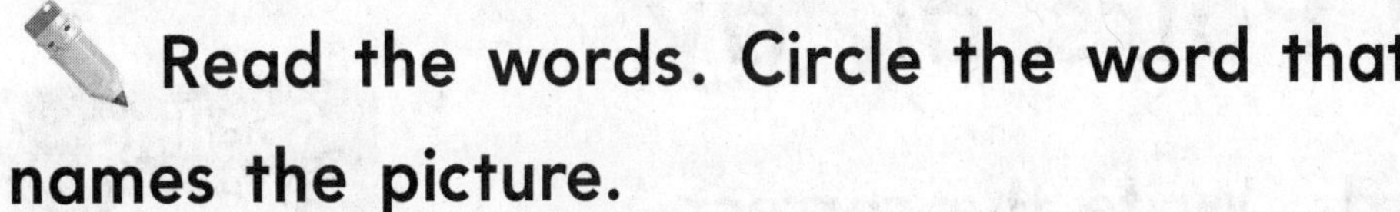

Read the words. Circle the word that names the picture.

1. 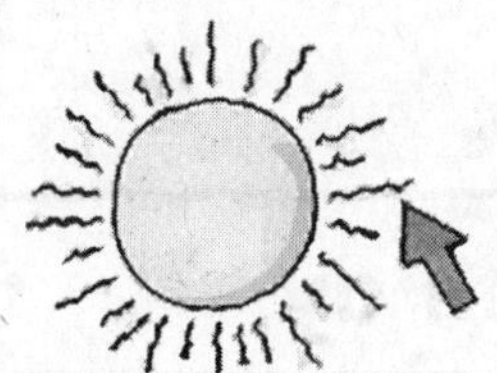

tray ray

---

2. 

sail tail

---

3. 

may play

---

4. 

rain main

---

5. 

paint pant

Name ______________________________

Spelling Words with the Vowel Pairs *ai*, *ay*

Sort the words. Write the correct Spelling Words in each column.

Spelling Words

play
grain
sail
mail
may
rain
way
day
stay
pain

Words with ai	Words with ay

Name ______________________________

Months, Days, and Holidays

Listen to the names in the Word Bank. Read along. Circle the month, day, or holiday in each sentence. Write it correctly on the line.

Word Bank

Labor Day   Tuesday   May   June   Saturday   August

1. On labor day we had a picnic. ____________

2. On tuesday Hank makes a cake. ____________

3. We plant seeds each may. ____________

Draw a line under the correct sentence in each pair.

4. Ike likes June for planting beans.
   Ike likes june for planting beans.

5. I picked beans on Saturday.
   I picked beans on saturday.

6. Peaches grow best in august.
   Peaches grow best in August.

Name ______________________

Using Different Kinds of Sentences

Write a friendly letter about a special meal you had. Write statements and a question.

____

Dear ______________________,

______________________ ______________________

I ate ______________________ with ______________________.

____

______________________.

(statement)

____

______________________.

(statement)

____

______________________?

(question)

______________________,

____

Name ___________________________

Contractions *'ll, 'd*

Write a word from the box to finish the sentence.

I'd

he'd	she'll	I'd	they'll	we'd

1. Ben said that ______________ be late today.

2. Beth said ______________ go to the beach.

3. Mom and Dad said ______________ go out at five.

4. Gus said, "______________ like to play in the sand."

5. We think ______________ like a day at the beach.

Name ________________________________

Where Does Food Come From?
Comprehension: Author's Purpose

Author's Purpose

Use the Inference Map to write details, and then tell the author's purpose.

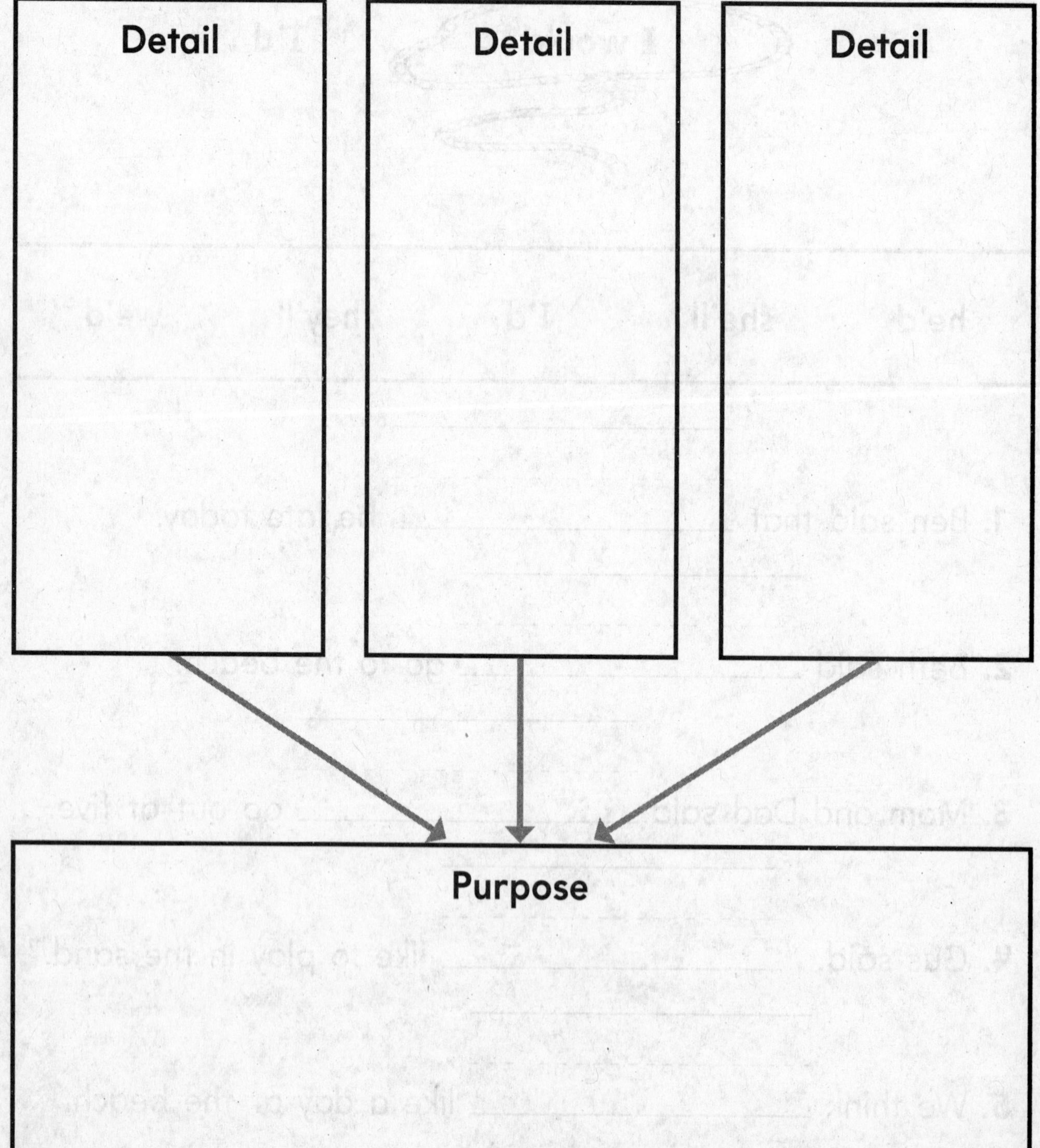

Name ______________________

Spelling Words with the Vowel Pairs *ai*, *ay*

Spelling Words

- play
- grain
- sail
- mail
- may
- rain
- way
- day
- stay
- pain

Write the Spelling Words that rhyme with fail.

1. ______________ 2. ______________

Write the Spelling Words that rhyme with bay.

3. ______________ 4. ______________

5. ______________ 6. ______________

7. ______________

Write the Spelling Words that rhyme with main.

8. ______________ 9. ______________ 10. ______________

Name ______________________________

Commas in Dates

Listen to the names of months in the Word Bank. Read along. Circle the comma in each date.

Word Bank

March April May June October

1. Ms. Ray moved to the farm on October 25, 2001.
2. She planted wheat on March 13, 2002.
3. She got some chicks on May 28, 2004.
4. She had eggs for sale on June 4, 2007.

The date in each sentence is underlined. Write the date correctly.

5. This patch was planted on March 16 2006.

____

6. The peas were planted on April 23 2007.

____

Name ______________________________

Planning My Letter

Write and draw details that tell what happened first, next, and last.

I will write my letter to ______________________.

I will tell about ______________________.

First

Next

Last

Name ______________________________

Spelling Words with the Long *a* Sound

Write the correct word to complete each sentence.

1. Can you come out and ______________?

   play **clay**

2. In April there is a lot of ______________.

   rake **rain**

3. Let us ______________ on the lake.

   sail **tail**

4. I feel a ______________ in my leg.

   train **pain**

5. Wheat is a ______________.

   grain **green**

Name ______________________________

Spiral Review

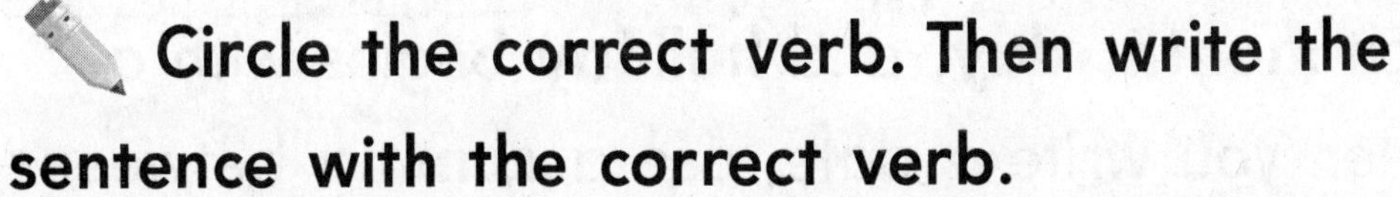

Circle the correct verb. Then write the sentence with the correct verb.

1. The kids (walk, walks) around the pond.

____

2. Nine sheep (eat, eats) the grass.

____

3. Ducks (flap, flaps) their wings.

____

4. One mule (sleep, sleeps) in the hay.

____

5. Pigs (play, plays) in the mud.

____

Name ________________________________

Grammar in Writing

The name of each **month, day,** and **holiday** begins with a capital letter. When you write a date, use a **comma** between the day of the month and the year.

Example:

labor day is monday september 7 2009.

Listen to the names of months and holidays in the Word Bank. Read along. Fix the mistakes in these sentences. Use proofreading marks.

Word Bank

July **August** **September** **October**
December **New Year's Eve**

1. In october it was cold.
2. Mr. Potts left on august 22 2004.
3. Every september they sell jam.
4. Ms. Down opened the shop on july 18 2007.
5. new year's eve is on december 31.

Proofreading Marks			
∧	Add	≡	Capital letter

Name ____________________

Words to Know

Listen to the clues. Read along. Circle the best answer to each clue.

1. This means **finished.**	paper	done
2. This is in a short while.	soon	great
3. This means **speak.**	were	talk
4. **Awful** is its opposite.	great	soon
5. A joke makes you do this.	laugh	done
6. You write on this.	work	paper
7. This is a **job.**	great	work
8. Past for **are.**	laugh	were

Name ______________________________

Words with *oa*, *ow*

Read the word. Circle the picture that matches the word.

1. boat

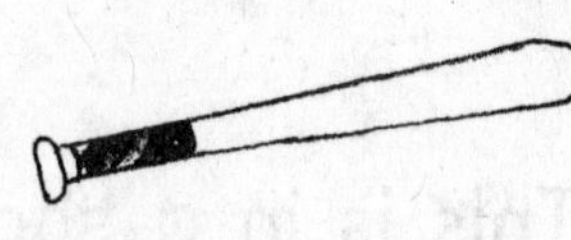

2. crow

3. goat

4. bowl

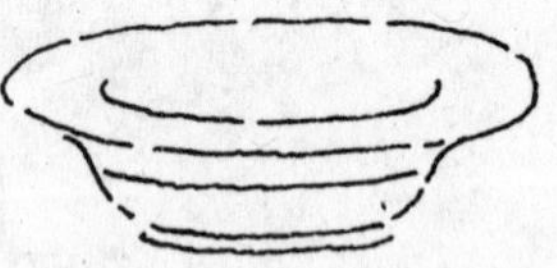
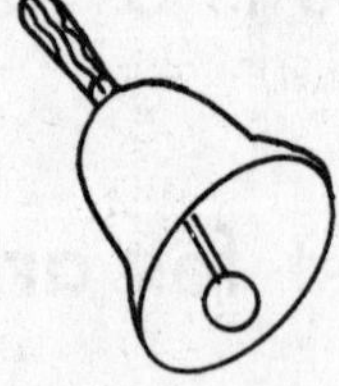

5. loaf

Name ____________________

Words with *oa*, *ow*

Circle the two words in each row that rhyme. Then write the letters that spell the long o sound.

1.	grow	blow	block	gray	___ ___
2.	slow	sling	throw	thick	___ ___
3.	much	road	load	lunch	___ ___
4.	coat	got	goat	long	___ ___
5.	flame	show	ground	snow	___ ___

Name ______________________________

Spelling Words with Vowel Pairs *oa*, *ow*

Sort the words. Write the correct Spelling Words in each column.

Words with ow	Words with oa

Spelling Words

show
row
boat
blow
toad
road
low
coat
grow
snow

Name ____________________

Future Using *will*

Circle the sentences that tell about the future. Rewrite the other sentences to tell about the future using *will*.

1. I read each day.

2. Brent will meet you at the shop.

3. My dad helps me read.

4. They washed the van.

5. Fran will beat the eggs.

6. ____________________

7. ____________________

8. ____________________

Name ______________________

Order of Events

Tomás Rivera
Writing: Write to Narrate

Draw pictures to show what you did to get ready for school today.

Write sentences about what you did to get ready for school today.

First, ______________________

Next, ______________________

Last, ______________________

Name ______________________

Contractions *'ve, 're*

Draw a line from each pair of words to its contraction.

You are	You're
They have	I've
I have	We're
We are	They've

Write the contraction from above that finishes each sentence.

1. ______________ all set for our big game.

2. ______________ my best friend.

3. ______________ had a lot of fun today!

4. ______________ had a lot of rain.

Name

Conclusions

Use the Inference Map to write three story details about Tomás Rivera's life. Then draw a conclusion that tells how he came to be who he is.

Detail	Detail	Detail

Conclusion

Name ________________________________

Spelling Words with Vowel Pairs *oa*, *ow*

Write the Spelling Word that fits each clue.

1. Opposite of **high** ____________

2. Another word for **street** ____________

3. You watch this on TV. ____________

4. You see this in winter. ____________

5. Wear this in the cold. ____________

6. An animal ____________

Spelling Words

- show
- row
- grow
- low
- blow
- snow
- boat
- coat
- road
- toad

Name ____________________

Future Using *going to*

Circle the sentences that tell about the future. Rewrite the other sentences to tell about the future. Use **going to** in each one.

1. I work with Ed.
2. Ed is going to have many crops.
3. My dad planted beets.
4. They pulled the weeds.
5. Jen is going to pick beans with Sam.
6. Tess has a pet cat.

7. ____________________
8. ____________________
9. ____________________
10. ____________________

Name ______________________________

Tomás Rivera
Spelling: Words with Long *o*

Spelling Words with the Long *o* Sound

Write the correct word to complete each sentence.

1. The class will put on a ______________ .

show **snow**

2. The ______________ hopped on the grass.

toad **load**

3. How do plants ______________ ?

throw **grow**

4. The ______________ came in with fish.

boat **bat**

5. Which ______________ will you sit in?

row **read**

Name ______________________________

Spiral Review

Notice the clue word yesterday that tells about the past. Circle the verb that tells about the past. Then write those verbs.

1. **Yesterday** mom (works, worked) at the new shop. ______________
2. She (opens, opened) the shop at nine. ______________
3. Many kids (walk, walked) into the shop. ______________
4. Val (asks, asked) for a new game. ______________
5. Her mom (helps, helped) her. ______________

Name ____________________

Planning My Personal Narrative

Draw and write details that tell what happened first, next, and last.

My Topic: ____________________

First

Next

Last

Grammar in Writing

You can write sentences that tell what may happen in the future. Use **will** or **is going to** to write sentences about the future.

Example: Jill walks.
Jill **will** walk.
Jill **is going to** walk.

Rewrite each sentence to tell about the future.

1. Tom runs far.

____

2. He went to work.

____

3. Grandpa sails his boat.

____

____

Name ______________________________

Words to Know

Circle the best answer to each question.

1. What word goes with **less**? **more** **use**

2. What word goes with **dry**? **door** **wash**

3. What word goes with **open**? **want** **door**

4. What word goes with **father**? **mother** **more**

5. What word goes with **new**? **old** **wash**

6. What word goes with **need**? **wash** **want**

7. What word goes with **test**? **more** **try**

8. What word goes with **tools**? **use** **mother**

Name ____________________

Compound Words

Name each picture. Circle two words to make a compound for the picture. Write the compound word.

1. sea pea nut side ____________________

2. trail rain bow mix ____________________

3. blue sea bird shell ____________________

4. snow mail box flake ____________________

5. cup sail cake boat ____________________

Name ______________________________

Compound Words

Choose words from the box to make a compound word to name each picture. Write the word. You will use some words more than once.

mail	rain	sail	sand	bow
row	boat	coat	box	

1. 

2. 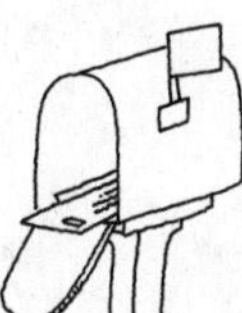

3. 

4. 

5. 

6. 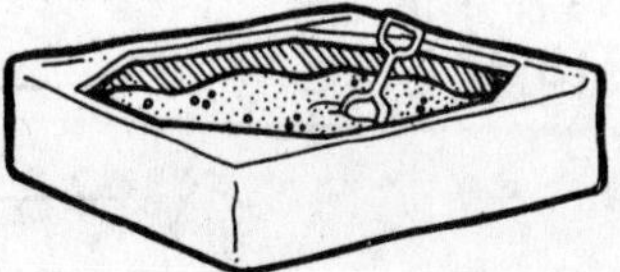

Name ______________________________

Spelling Compound Words

Write the two words that make up each Spelling Word shown below.

1. bedtime ____________ ____________
2. himself ____________ ____________
3. flagpole ____________ ____________
4. sailboat ____________ ____________
5. backpack ____________ ____________
6. sunset ____________ ____________
7. raincoat ____________ ____________

Name ______________________________

Prepositional Phrases for Where

Circle the prepositional phase in each sentence. Write it on the line.

1. Rabbit went to Squirrel's home.

____

2. He went up the steps.

____

3. He knocked on the door.

____

Complete each sentence. Write a prepositional phrase that tells where.

4. The rabbit lives ______________________________.

5. The rabbit hopped ______________________________.

Name ______________________________

Exact Details

Little Rabbit's Tale
Writing: Write to Narrate

Read each underlined detail. Write a more exact detail to finish each sentence.

1. I watched an animal.

I watched ______________________.

2. I fed it some food.

I fed it ______________________.

3. It moved around.

It ______________________.

4. I will teach it something.

I will teach it ______________________.

Name ______________________________

Little Rabbit's Tale
Phonics: Short *e* Sound Spelled *ea*

Words with Short Vowel /ĕ/*ea*

Circle two words that have the short e sound.

1.	red	bread	bat	rode
2.	sled	bone	robe	head
3.	bed	dead	cube	lot
4.	peach	fed	Fred	drink
5.	led	paint	loaf	thread

Name ____________________

Cause and Effect

Think of three events from the story that are causes and three that are effects. Write them in the chart.

What Happened?	Why Did It Happen?

Name ____

Spelling Compound Words

Draw a line from a word on the left to a word on the right to make each Spelling Word.

1. bath	time
2. flag	tub
3. bed	pole
4. sun	pack
5. back	set
6. play	coat
7. rain	pen
8. sail	side
9. in	self
10. him	boat

Spelling Words

- bedtime
- sunset
- bathtub
- sailboat
- flagpole
- backpack
- playpen
- raincoat
- inside
- himself

Name ______________________________

Prepositional Phrases

Circle the prepositional phrase in each sentence. Decide if the prepositional phrase tells where or when. Write where or when on the line.

1. The friends play after lunch. ______________

2. They meet at Viv's home. ______________

3. Viv swings under a tree. ______________

4. Lin skips on the grass. ______________

5. Mom comes home at five o'clock. ______________

6. Lin goes home before then. ______________

Name ____________________

Spelling Compound Words

Write the correct word to complete each sentence.

1. The ____________________ was very red.

   sunset **himself**

2. Let us play ____________________ today.

   inside **flagpole**

3. I carry my ____________________ with me.

   playpen **backpack**

4. Before ____________________ I brush my teeth.

   bedtime **sailboat**

5. My ____________________ has a matching hat.

   bathtub **raincoat**

Name ______________________________

Spiral Review

Write each sentence with the correct verb.

1. This puppet (is, are) small.

2. Raindrops (is, are) wet.

3. The lambs (is, are) white.

4. The show (was, were) funny.

5. Those muffins (was, were) huge.

Name ____________________

Grammar in Writing

A prepositional phrase can tell when or where.

Example:	We walk **after lunch**.	when
	We walk **in the park**.	where

Add a prepositional phrase to each sentence to tell when or where. Write the new sentence on the line.

1. My friends and I ran.

____

2. Something fell.

____

3. I tripped.

____

4. I went home.

____

Name ______________________________

Words to Know

Circle the correct word to complete each sentence.

1. Ben (night, saw) the new slide today.

2. This swing is (better, saw) than that swing.

3. The green leaves (turned, told) yellow and red.

4. Nan (window, thought) about what to bake.

5. Dad's car is getting (saw, pretty) old.

6. Some animals hunt at (night, pretty).

7. Close your (better, window) when it rains.

8. Jen (told, thought) us about her trip.

Name ____________________

Words with *ar*

Circle the word that matches the picture.

1.

cat card

2.

star stamp

3.

march much

4.

barn bark

5.

arm art

6.

yard yarn

Name ______________________

Words with *ar*

The Tree
Phonics: *r*-Controlled Vowel

Look at the picture and read the words. Write the word that matches the picture.

1.

stem start

2.

cat cart

3.

car card

4.

shake shark

5.

pack park

Name ______________________

Spelling Words with *r*-Controlled Vowel *ar*

Spelling Words

far
arm
yard
art
jar
bar
barn
bark
card
yarn

Write the Spelling Words that rhyme with far, yard, and barn.

1. **Far** rhymes with ______________________

and ______________________.

2. **Yard** rhymes with ______________________.

3. **Barn** rhymes with ______________________.

Write the Spelling Word that names the picture.

4. 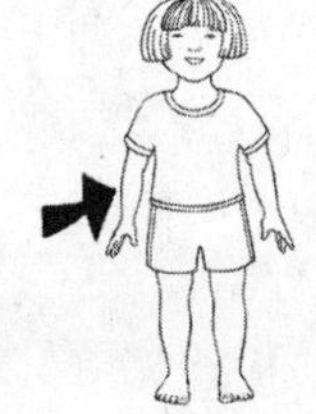

____

5. 

____

6. 

____

Pronouns That Name One

Circle the pronoun that can take the place of the underlined word or words.

1. Grandpa makes a shed.

   He **She** **It**

2. The shed is short and wide.

   He **She** **It**

3. Ann helps Grandpa work in the shed.

   He **She** **It**

Write He, She, or It to take the place of the underlined word or words.

4. Joe sees a nest.

   ______________ sees a nest.

5. The nest has eggs.

   ______________ has eggs.

Name ______________________________

Dialogue

Name another animal that Poppleton could have asked about his tree. Then write what the two characters might have said.

Poppleton still did not know what to do with his tree.

He asked ____________________ what to do.

" ______________________________

____

______________________________ ?" Poppleton asked.

" ______________________________

____

______________________________ ," said his friend.

Name ______________________________

The Tree
Phonics: *r*-Controlled Vowel *or, ore*

Words with *or, ore*

Read the sentences. Circle the sentence that tells about the picture.

1. We look at the score.

We look at the star.

2. I like to do chores.

I snore when I sleep.

3. She finds shells at the shore.

She finds fish at the shop.

4. He can play the thorn.

He can play the horn.

5. Here is a jar.

Here is a fork.

Name ______________________

Story Structure

Write or draw pictures to show the characters, setting, and plot of the story.

Characters	Setting

Plot
Beginning
Middle
End

Name ___

Spelling Words with *r*-Controlled Vowel *ar*

Write the Spelling Word that names the picture.

Spelling Words

far
arm
yard
art
jar
bar
barn
bark
card
yarn

1.

___

2.

___

3.

___

4.

___

5.

___

6.

___

Name ______________________________

Pronouns That Name More Than One

Circle the pronoun that can take the place of each underlined subject.

1. Workers plant trees in the park.

   We **They**

2. The trees grow big.

   We **They**

3. Sis and I sit under the trees.

   We **They**

Write We or They to take the place of each underlined subject.

4. Dad and I walk to the park.

   ______________ walk to the park.

5. Pete and Kate run and play.

   ______________ run and play.

Name ____________________

Planning My Sentences

Write and draw details that tell what happened first and next.

Topic: After Poppleton and Cherry Sue watched the ____________________ birds, they ____________________.

First

Next

Name ______________________

Spelling Words with *r*-Controlled Vowel *ar*

Write the correct word to complete each sentence.

fun far

1. She lives __________ away from me.

ants arm

2. He waves his __________ in the air.

yard yarn

3. We play in the __________.

art part

4. We paint in __________ class.

bar jar

5. She gave me a __________ of jam.

card bar

6. Hang your coats on the __________.

barn big

7. The sheep are in the __________.

Name ____________________

Spiral Review

Draw a line under each question.

1. What sort of tree is this?
2. Do all trees have leaves?
3. Pine trees have cones.
4. What animals live in trees?
5. Birds live in trees.
6. Do we need trees?
7. Trees give us air.
8. Do we get food from trees?

Name ______________________________

Grammar in Writing

The pronouns **he, she,** and **it** name one. The pronouns **we** and **they** name more than one.

Fix the mistakes in the sentences. Use proofreading marks.

Example: The shed is done. ~~She~~ It looks nice.

1. Mom saws. He makes a shelf for the shed.

2. Bob and I get paint. They paint the shelf.

3. Mom has some grapes. It puts them in a bowl.

4. My friends come over. We want to see the shed.

Proofreading Marks	
∧	add
⌒ (delete mark)	take out

Name ______________________________

Words to Know

Circle the word that best completes each sentence.

1. I like (until, learning) about animals.

2. Our dog Pip is five (follow, years) old.

3. Pip has (baby, eight) new pups.

4. She will feed her pups (until, learning) they are older.

5. A (eight, young) kitten came to our home.

6. The new kitten likes to (until, follow) Pip.

7. The kitten (begins, learning) to think he is Pip's pup!

8. The new kitten is not Pip's (years, baby).

Name ______________________________

Lesson 22
PRACTICE BOOK

Amazing Animals
Phonics: *r*-Controlled Vowels
er, ir, ur

Words with *er*, *ir*, *ur*

Read the word. Circle the picture that matches the word.

1.	bird	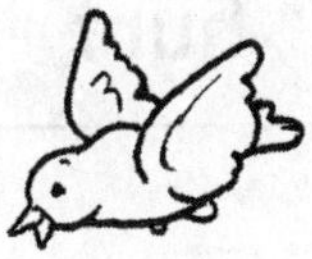	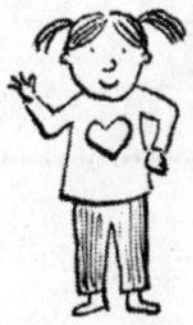
2.	turn	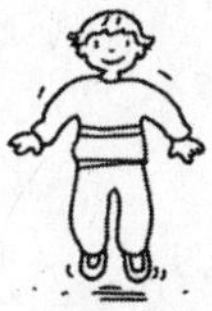	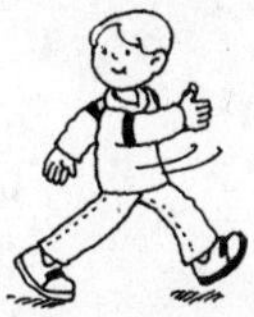
3.	her	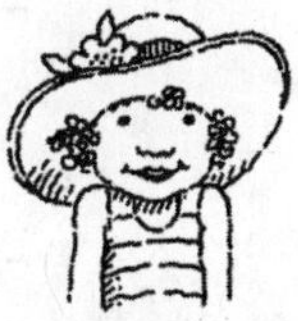	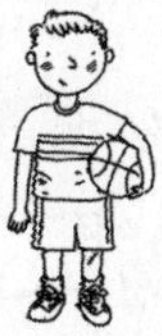
4.	burn	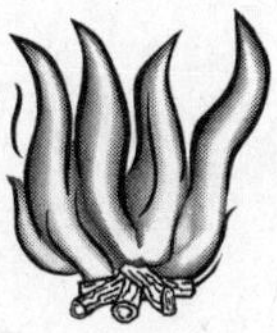	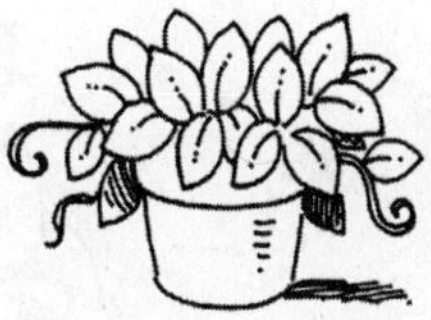
5.	third	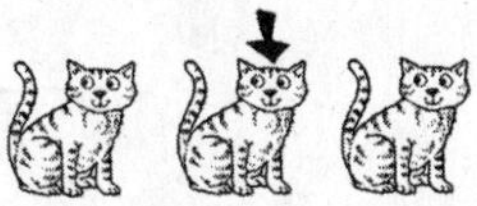	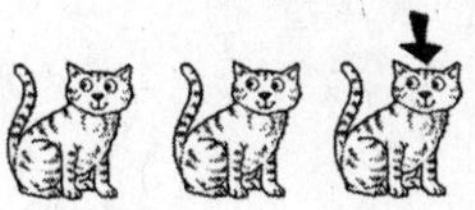
6.	herd	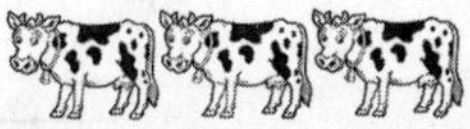	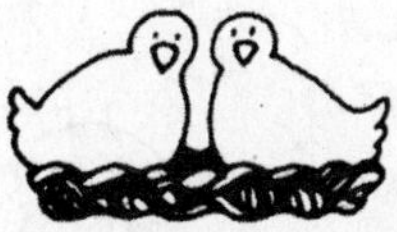

Name ______________________________

Words with *er*, *ir*, *ur*

Amazing Animals
Phonics: *r*-Controlled Vowels
er, *ir*, *ur*

Read the words in the box. Write the word that matches the picture.

clerk	shirt	stir	hurt	curl

1. ______________________

2. ______________________

3. ______________________

4. ______________________

5. ______________________

Name ______________________________

Spelling Words with *r*-Controlled Vowels *er, ir, ur*

Spelling Words

sir
fern
girl
her
third
hurt
fur
bird
turn
stir

Write the Spelling Words with er.

1. ______________ 2. ______________

Write the Spelling Words with ir.

3. ______________ 4. ______________

5. ______________ 6. ______________

7. ______________

Write the Spelling Words with ur.

8. ______________ 9. ______________

10. ______________

Name ______________________________

Naming Yourself Last

Circle the correct words to finish each sentence.

1. ______ see the goat.

   Jean and i   Jean and I

2. ______ pet the sheep.

   I and Steve   Steve and I

3. ______ look at the ducks.

   Rex and I   i and Rex

Write the words from the word box to finish the sentence.

Ann	I

4. ______________ and ______________ hold the baby snakes.

Name ______________________________

Exact Verbs

Draw a picture of an animal for a story. Give your animal a name.

Name: ______________________________

Finish these story sentences about your animal. Use exact verbs.

______________ is a ______________ .
name kind of animal

______________ likes to ______________ .
name exact verb

______________ always ______________ a lot!
name exact verb

Name ____________________

Words with *er, ir, ur*

Choose a word from the box to name each picture. Write the word.

girl	turn	chirp	third	hers	dirt

1. ____________________

2. ____________________

3. ____________________

4. ____________________

5. ____________________

6. ____________________

Name ____________________

Conclusions

Write three details from the story. Then write a conclusion telling in what way you think the animals are the same.

Detail	Detail	Detail

Conclusion

Name ______________________________

Spelling Words with *r*-Controlled Vowels *er*, *ir*, *ur*

Write the Spelling Word that fits each clue.

1. Opposite of **boy** ____________
2. Goes with **pain** ____________
3. What a bear has ____________
4. Goes with **three** ____________
5. Opposite of **him** ____________
6. An animal ____________

Spelling Words

her
fern
girl
sir
stir
bird
fur
hurt
turn
third

Name ____________________

Naming Yourself with *I*

Write the sentences correctly.

1. Jay and me visit a farm.

____

2. Me and Bree feed the ducks.

____

3. Dave and me pet the sheep.

____

4. Me and Ed see the lambs.

____

5. Meg and me hold the cat.

____

Name ____

Planning My Sentences

Write and draw details that tell what happened first and next.

My Topic: I will write about a

____

First

Next

Name ______________________________

Spelling Words with *r*-Controlled Vowels *er*, *ir*, *ur*

Amazing Animals
Spelling: Words with *r*-Controlled Vowels *er, ir, ur*

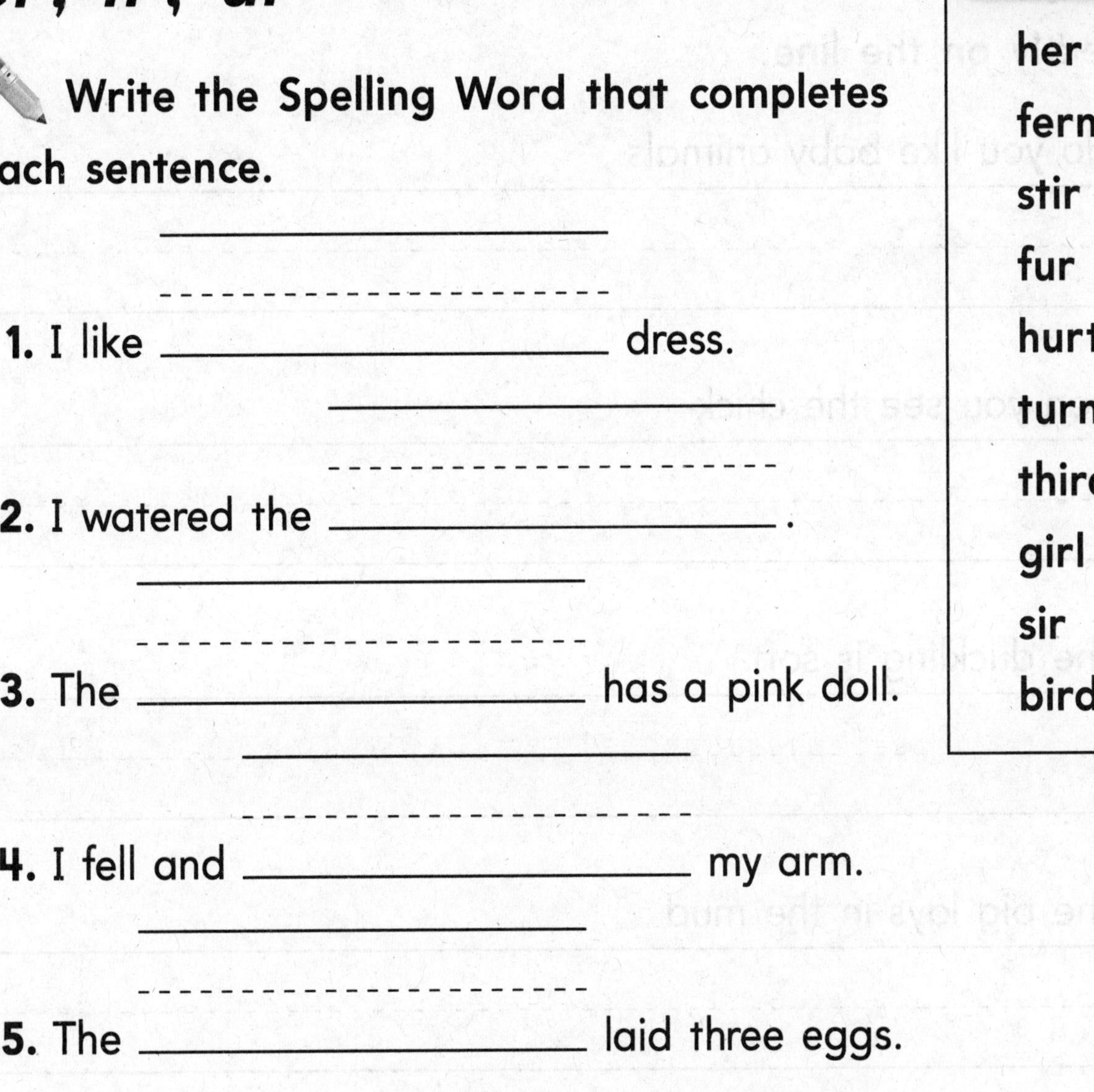

Write the Spelling Word that completes each sentence.

1. I like ______________ dress.
2. I watered the ______________.
3. The ______________ has a pink doll.
4. I fell and ______________ my arm.
5. The ______________ laid three eggs.
6. The cat has thick ______________.

Spelling Words

her
fern
stir
fur
hurt
turn
third
girl
sir
bird

Name ____________________

Spiral Review

Decide if each sentence is a statement or a question. Then write the sentence correctly on the line.

1. do you like baby animals

2. can you see the chick

3. the duckling is soft

4. the pig lays in the mud

5. how old is the cub

Name ____________________

Grammar in Writing

Use the **pronoun I** in the subject of a sentence. Name yourself last.

Fix the mistakes in these sentences. Use proofreading marks.

Example: ~~Me~~ Ted and ~~Ted~~ I see the ducklings.

1. I and Mark feed the pups.

2. Jon and me pet the baby calf.

3. Me and Hing look at the piglets.

4. Kris and i see the baby birds.

Proofreading Marks	
∧	add
℘	take out
≡	capital letter

Name ______________________________

Words to Know

Circle the word that best completes each sentence.

1. We can go to the play (together, boy).

2. The box has (began, nothing) in it.

3. The new (boy, along) is named Dan.

4. Dan and his (together, father) like to fish.

5. My (house, nothing) has a blue door.

6. Jan skipped (house, along) the path.

7. I will sing the song (again, boy).

8. A bell (house, began) to ring.

Name ____

Whistle for Willie
Phonics: Vowel digraph *oo (book)*

The Vowel Sound *oo* *(book)*

Circle the word that matches the picture.

1.

book hook

2.

book cook

3.

wool wood

4.

hook hood

5.

brook took

6.

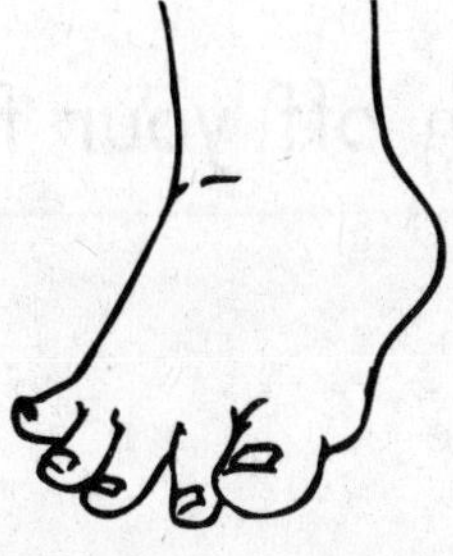

soot foot

Name ___________________________________

Whistle for Willie
Phonics: Vowel digraph *oo (book)*

Words with *oo (book)*

Circle the sentence that matches the picture.

1. We cook at mealtime.

We look at the time.

2. I see a little brook.

I see a little book.

3. He has a hat made of wool.

He has a box made of wood.

4. Put your coat on a hook.

Put your coat in a hood.

5. Wash off that soot.

Wash off your foot.

Name ________________________________

Whistle for Willie
Spelling: Words with *oo*

Spelling Words with Vowel Digraph *oo*

Sort the words. Write the correct Spelling Words in each column.

Spelling Words

- look
- book
- good
- hook
- brook
- took
- foot
- shook
- wood
- hood

Words with ook	Words with ood

Name ______________________________

Using *my*, *your*, *his*, and *her*

Write the correct pronoun to finish each sentence.

1. I hug ____________ dog Mags.

   me **my**

2. Mags runs after ____________ stick.

   her **she**

3. Rick brings ____________ dog.

   he **his**

4. You can bring ____________ dog, too.

   your **you**

5. We can play in ____________ backyard!

   they **my**

Name ______________________

Order of Events

Finish the sentences. Give a summary of the first part of **Whistle for Willie.**

Peter wished ______________________.

He tried ______________________.

When Peter saw Willie, he ______________________
______________________.

Then, Willie ______________________
______________________.

Name ______________________________

How Many Syllables?

Read each word. Circle how many syllables it has. Hint: Each time you hear a vowel sound, there is a syllable.

1. hammer

1 2

2. doctor

1 2

3. stood

1 2

4. rabbit

1 2

5. mister

1 2

6. third

1 2

Name ______________________________

Cause and Effect

Use the chart to tell what happens in the story and why it happens.

What Happens?	Why Did It Happen?

Name ______________________________

Spelling Words with Vowel Digraph *oo*

Write each group of Spelling Words in ABC order.

look	hood	shook	hook
good	wood	foot	brook
book		took	

______________	______________
______________	______________
______________	______________
______________	______________
______________	______________

Spelling Words

look
book
good
hook
brook
took
foot
shook
wood
hood

Name ________________________________

Using *mine*, *yours*, *his*, and *hers*

Write the correct pronoun to finish each sentence.

1. This mitt is ______________.

   your yours

2. The bat is ______________.

   he his

3. That treat is ______________.

   you yours

4. This house is ______________.

   my mine

5. That dog is ______________.

   hers her

Name ______________________

Planning My Summary

Write sentences and draw details for your summary of Whistle for Willie.

My Topic: ______________________

Name ______________________________

Spelling Words with the *oo* Sound in *book*

Spelling Words

- book
- look
- good
- hook
- brook
- foot
- took
- shook
- wood
- hood

Write the Spelling Words that make sense in each sentence.

1. Can I ____________ at your ____________?

2. I ____________ the ____________ off his coat.

3. I put my ____________ in the ____________.

Name ____________________

Spiral Review

Listen to the names of months in the Word Bank. Read along. Write each date correctly.

Word Bank

February **March** **August** **October** **December**

1. The pet shop opened on march 13 1999.

2. Lisa got a cat on february 22 2007.

3. My dog had pups on august 1 2008.

4. His dog won a prize on october 25 2009.

5. My dog got a new bowl on december 22 2010.

Name ____________________

Grammar in Writing

- Some pronouns show that something belongs to someone.
- The pronouns **my**, **your**, **his**, and **her** come before a noun.
- The pronouns **mine**, **yours**, **his**, and **hers** come at the end of a sentence.

 **Fix the mistakes in these sentences. Use proofreading marks.**

Example: The dog is ~~he~~ his.

1. I play with mine dog.

2. That is hers bowl.

3. This leash is your.

4. Jack has a new dog. The dog is hers.

Proofreading Marks	
∧	add
——ℓ	take out

Name ______________________________

Words to Know

Write a word from the box to complete each sentence.

Words to Know
- also
- anything
- flower
- kind
- places
- ready
- upon
- warm

1. I want to pick the ______________ .
2. It is very ______________ outside.
3. Cats sleep in soft ______________ .
4. Nate ______________ likes ice cream.
5. Tag is one ______________ of game.
6. Are you ______________ to go?
7. Lee reads ______________ about bugs.
8. I put the hat ______________ my head.

Name ______________________

A Butterfly Grows
Phonics: Vowel Digraphs *oo* *(moon), ou, ew*

Words with *oo (moon)*, *ou, ew*

Circle the word that names the picture.

1.

moth moon

2.

spoon spot

3.

scream screw

4.

soap soup

5.

boat boot

6.

stool stole

Name ______________________________

A Butterfly Grows
Phonics: Words with *oo (moon), ou, ew*

Words with *oo (moon)*, *ou, ew*

Write the word that best completes each sentence. Use the words in the Word Bank.

Word Bank

cool group room drew stool

1. I got together with a ______________ of friends.

2. We had fun playing in my ______________.

3. We ______________ some pictures and hung them up.

4. Then we painted my old ______________.

5. Now the room looks ______________!

Name ______________________________

A Butterfly Grows
Spelling: Words with *oo, ou, ew*

Spelling Words with Vowel Digraphs *oo*, *ou*, *ew*

Spelling Words

soon
new
noon
zoo
boot
too
moon
blew
soup
you

Write the Spelling Words with ou.

1. ______________ 2. ______________

Write the Spelling Words with ew.

3. ______________ 4. ______________

Write the Spelling Words with oo.

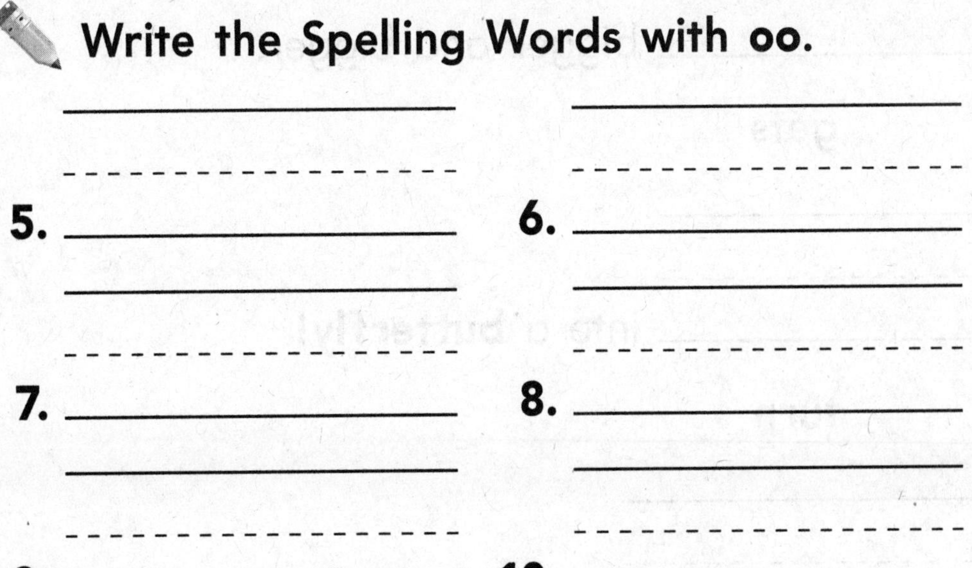

5. ______________ 6. ______________

7. ______________ 8. ______________

9. ______________ 10. ______________

Name ______________________________

Pronouns and Action Verbs

Write the correct verb to finish each sentence about a **caterpillar** and a **butterfly.**

1. Jill ______________ at the leaf.

   look **looks**

2. She ______________ a **caterpillar**.

   sees **see**

3. It ______________ bigger and bigger.

   get **gets**

4. It ______________ into a **butterfly!**

   turns **turn**

5. She ______________ her hands.

   clap **claps**

Name ______________________________

Describing Characters

Write clear details to finish the story.
Some details should describe Rex and Grace.

Rex was a ______________________ dog. He lived with

a ______________________ girl named Grace. Grace

wanted to teach Rex to ______________________ .

She told Rex to ______________________ . When Rex did

the trick, Grace told Rex, "______________________!"

Rex wagged his ______________________ tail.

Name ______________________________

Words with *ue*, *u*, *u_e*

Circle the two words in each row that have the same vowel sound. Write the letters that spell the sound.

				ue u u-e
1.	clue	trust	true	____ ____
2.	prune	flute	float	____ ____
3.	goal	flu	truth	____ ____
4.	tone	tune	rule	____ ____
5.	blue	blunt	glue	____ ____

Name ______________________________

Sequence of Events

Write about things that happen in **A Butterfly Grows**. Put the events in order.

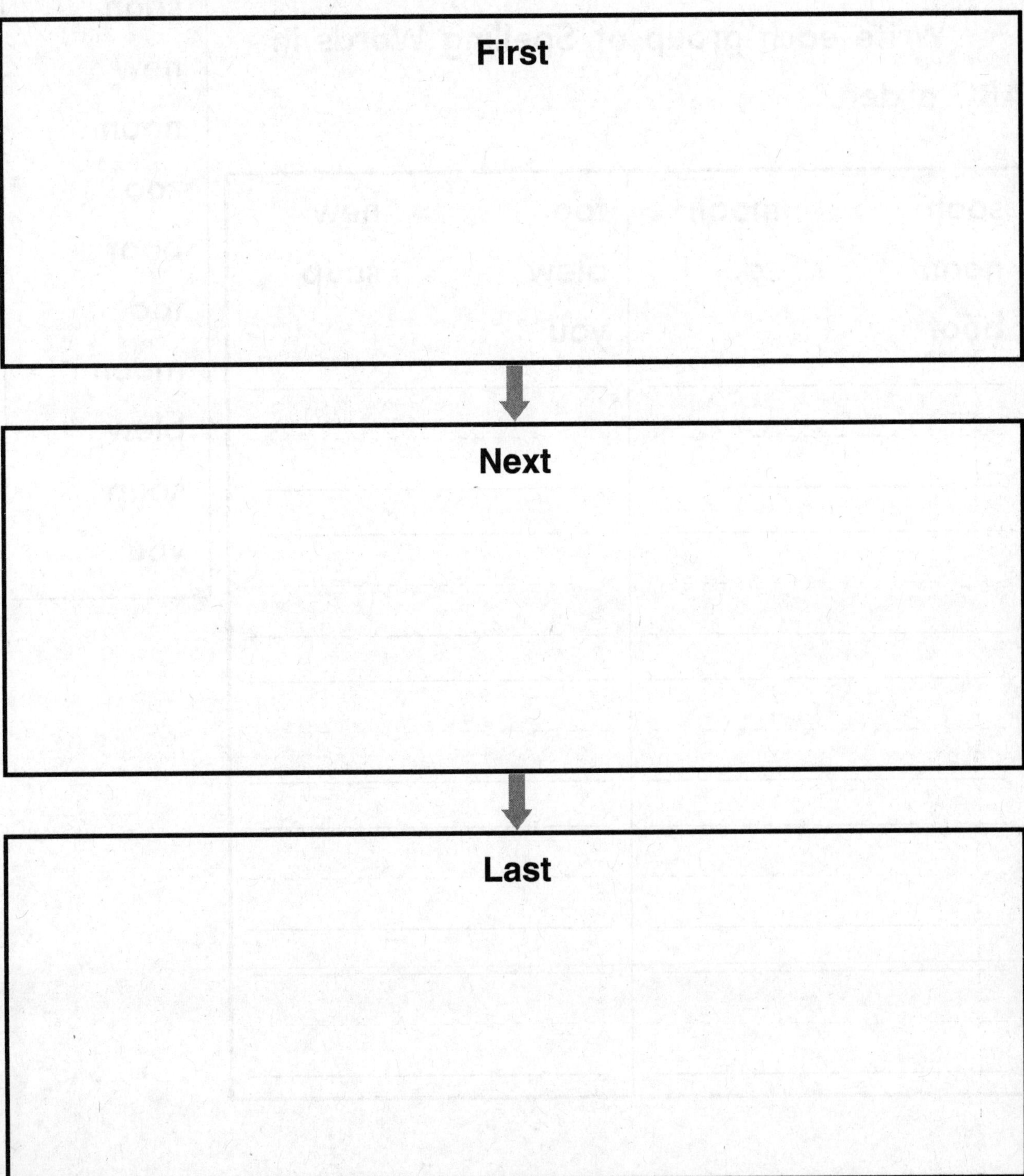

Name ____________________

Spelling Words with Vowel Digraphs *oo*, *ou*, *ew*

Spelling Words

soon
new
noon
zoo
boot
too
moon
blew
soup
you

Write each group of Spelling Words in ABC order.

soon moon noon zoo boot	too new blew soup you
____________________	____________________
____________________	____________________
____________________	____________________
____________________	____________________
____________________	____________________

Name ____________________

Pronouns and *be*

 **Write the correct verb to finish each sentence.**

1. She ____________ in the park.

   is **are**

2. I ____________ with her.

   is **am**

3. We ____________ sitting on rocks.

   is **are**

4. They ____________ warm.

   am **are**

5. It ____________ a nice day!

   is **are**

Name ______________________________

Spelling Words with the *oo* and *ew* Sound

Spelling Words

soon
new
noon
zoo
boot
too
moon
blew
soup
you

Write the Spelling Word that completes each sentence.

1. We will have our lunch at ______________ .

2. I hope that I will see you ______________ .

3. The wind ______________ the tree over.

4. I saw many animals at the ______________ .

5. There was a full ______________ last night.

6. It is ______________ hot to play outside.

7. We will have ______________ for lunch.

8. I need a ______________ pencil.

Name ___________________________

Spiral Review

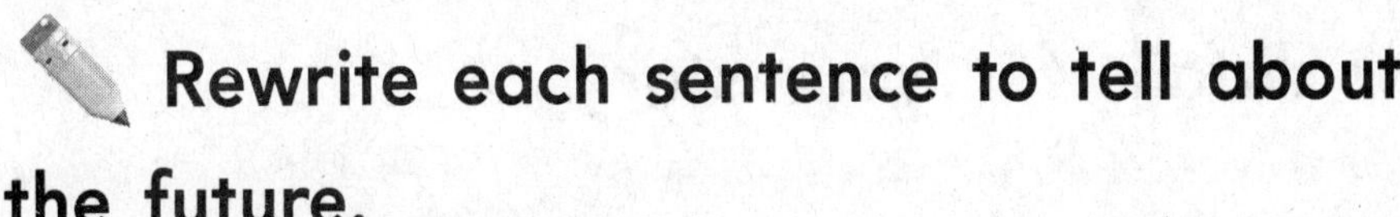

Rewrite each sentence to tell about the future.

1. It stopped raining.

2. I biked to the park.

3. We look for birds.

4. I watch from a bench.

5. A bird landed here.

Name ________________

A Butterfly Grows
Writing: Write to Express

Planning My Story

Write and draw details for your story.

Characters	Setting

Plot
Beginning
Middle
End

Name ______________________________

Grammar in Writing

- Add **s** to most **verbs** when they tell about a pronoun that names one.
- Use **am** with the pronoun **I**. Use **is** with pronouns that name one. Use **are** with pronouns that name more than one.

Fix the mistakes in these sentences. Use proofreading marks.

Example: We ~~is~~ ^**are** in the park.

1. We sees many flowers.

2. They am pretty.

3. I calls my friend.

4. She give me a big smile.

Proofreading Marks	
^	add
⌒	take out

Name ______________________________

Words to Know

Draw a line to match each picture to the word that goes with it.

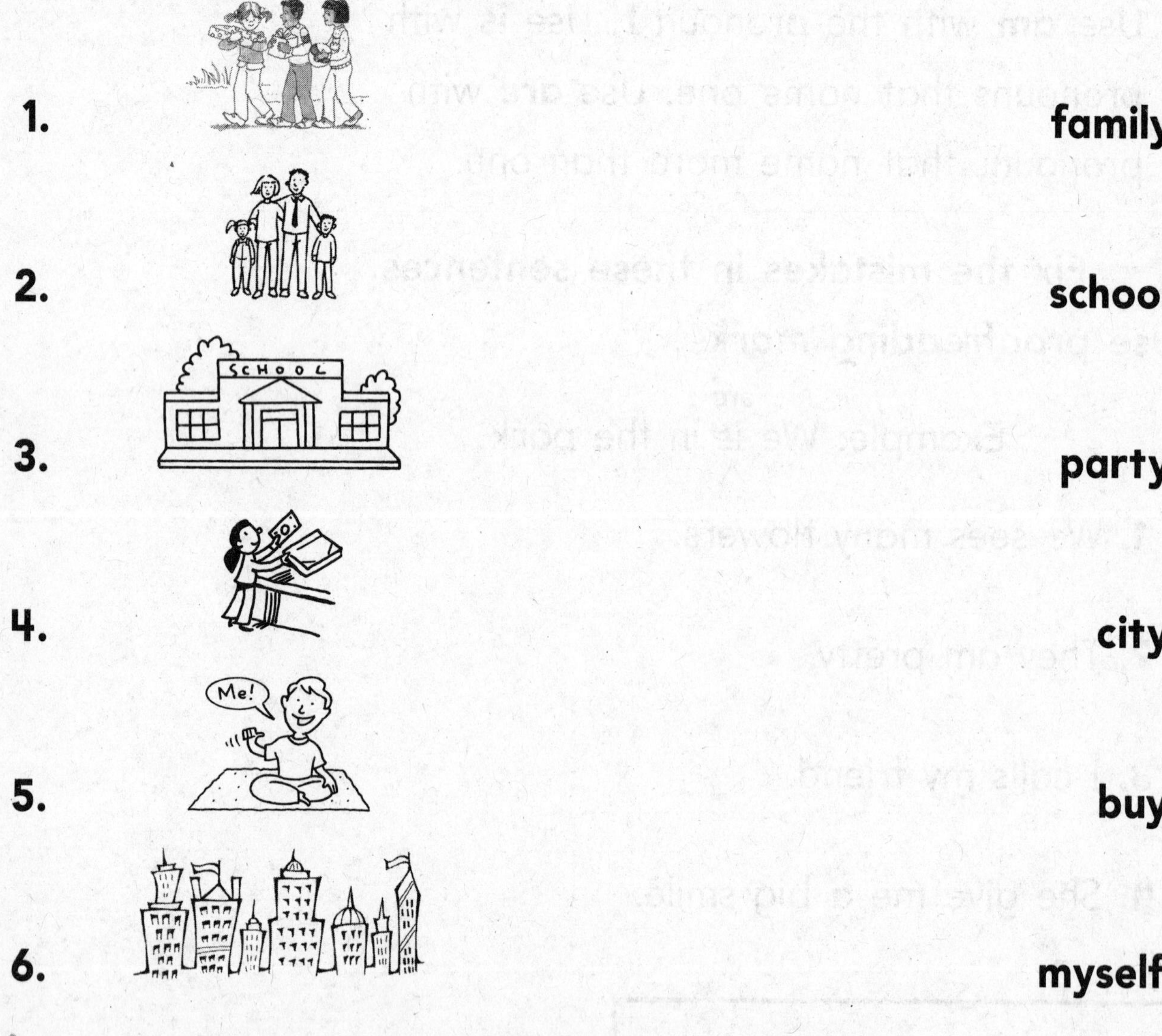

1.	**family**
2.	**school**
3.	**party**
4.	**city**
5.	**buy**
6.	**myself**

Use the words seven and please together in a sentence. Write it on the line.

____

Name ______________________________

Words with *ou, ow*

Circle the word that names the picture.

1.

cot cow

2.

couch coach

3.

moose mouse

4.

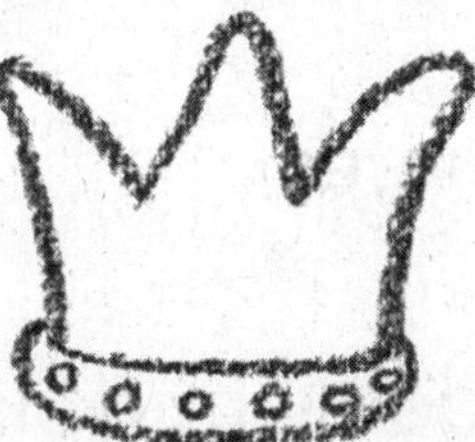

crow crown

5.

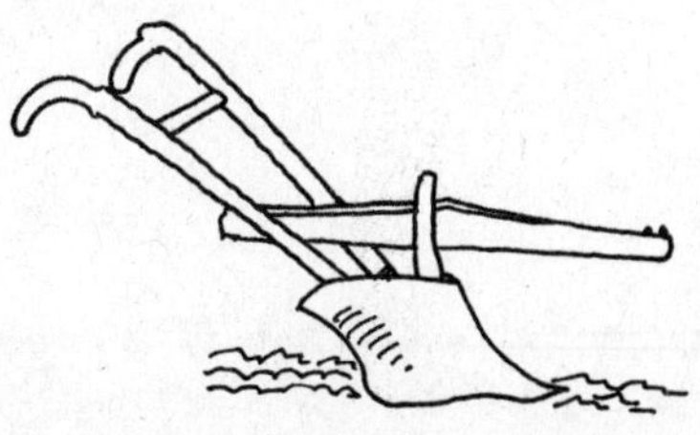

plate plow

6.

cloud closed

Name ______________________

Words with *ou, ow*

Circle the word that best completes each sentence.

1. I got a new pet. He's a ____ dog.

   hound **hold**

2. He should not jump up on the ____.

   coach **couch**

3. At night, my dog ____ at the moon.

   holes **howls**

4. My dog's bark is very ____.

   loud **load**

5. He will ____ when someone comes to the house!

   grow **growl**

6. He sits when I tell him to get ____.

   down **dome**

Name ______________________________

Spelling Words with Vowel Diphthongs *ow, ou*

Sort the words. Write the correct Spelling Words in each column.

Words with ou	Words with ow

Spelling Words

how
now
cow
owl
ouch
house
found
out
gown
town

Name ______________________________

Contractions with *not*

Write a contraction from the box for the underlined word or words.

Word Bank

isn't
aren't
can't
don't

1. This house is not empty now.

____

2. I do not know where my books are.

____

3. They are not in this big box.

____

4. I cannot find my jump rope.

____

5. I do not have a new friend yet.

____

Name ______________________________

The New Friend
Writing: Write to Express

Sentences with Different Lengths

Make long sentences by joining two short sentences with and.

1. Kirk moved to a new city. He was happy.

______________________________,
and ______________________________.

2. The city is far away. It is very big.

______________________________,
and ______________________________.

3. Kirk made new friends. He saw new places.

______________________________,
and ______________________________.

Name ______________________

Words with *oi*, *oy*, *au*, *aw*

Circle the two words in each row that have the same vowel sound. Write the letters that spell the sound.

		oi oy au aw
1.	coins coats join	____ ____
2.	joy boy book	____ ____
3.	house sauce pause	____ ____
4.	dune dawn crawl	____ ____
5.	point paint moist	____ ____

Name ______________________________

Understanding Characters

Write or draw things the boys said in the story in the **Speaking** box. Write or draw things the boys did in the **Acting** box. Write or draw about the feelings of the boys in the **Feeling** box.

Speaking	Acting	Feeling

Name ____________________

Spelling Words with Vowel Diphthongs *ou*, *ow*

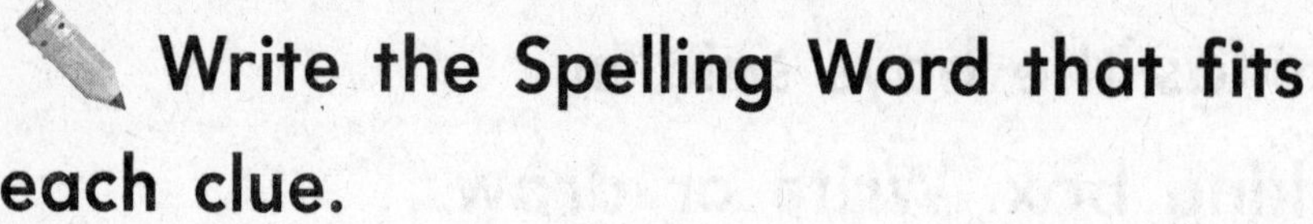

Write the Spelling Word that fits each clue.

Spelling Words

- how
- now
- cow
- owl
- ouch
- house
- found
- out
- gown
- town

1. Opposite of **later** ____________________
2. Opposite of **lost** ____________________
3. A farm animal ____________________
4. Smaller than a city ____________________
5. Opposite of **in** ____________________
6. A bird ____________________

Name ________________________________

Contractions with Pronouns

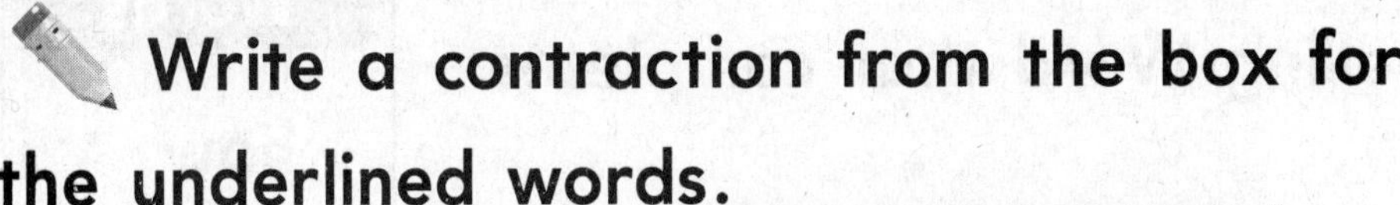

Write a contraction from the box for the underlined words.

Word Bank

I'm	he's	she's	it's

1. It is a pretty day.

____

2. I am going to school with my new friend.

____

3. He is in the car with his mom.

____

4. She is driving us.

____

Name ______________________________

The New Friend
Spelling: Words with *ow* and *ou*

Spelling Words with the *ow* and *ou* Sound

Write the Spelling Word that completes each sentence.

1. We're walking to my ______________.

2. ______________ will you get home?

3. Do you live far from ______________?

4. I'm going ______________ to play.

5. ______________! That hurt!

6. He's coming home right ______________.

Spelling Words

- how
- house
- now
- owl
- cow
- found
- town
- ouch
- out
- gown

Name ______________________________

Spiral Review

Circle the prepositional phrase in each sentence. Decide if the prepositional phrase tells where or when. Write where or when on the line.

1. Max and Viv play after school. ______________
2. They meet in the park. ______________
3. Viv's kite is stuck in a tree. ______________
4. They race on the grass. ______________
5. The park closes at five o'clock. ______________
6. The friends will meet again next week. ______________

Name ______________________________

Grammar in Writing

- A contraction is a short way of writing some words.
- This mark (') takes the place of missing letters.

Fix the mistakes in these sentences. Use proofreading marks.

Example: ~~H'es~~ in a new house. (He's)

1. Im' with my new friend.
2. Today shes putting her toys away.
3. She cant' find the games.
4. The books are'nt in the box.
5. We do'nt play today.

Proofreading Marks	
∧	add
‿୨	take out

Name ______________________________

Words to Know

Circle the correct word to complete each sentence.

1. A (even, teacher) helps you learn.

2. Please push that box (toward, pushed) me.

3. A (bear, surprised) is a big animal.

4. The lamp is (above, pushed) the shelf.

5. Mom (teacher, pushed) Kim on the swing.

6. Jim was (surprised, even) by his birthday gift.

7. All the family came, (even, above) Grandma.

8. Ben (toward, studied) the painting closely.

Name ______________________________

Adding *-ed*, *-ing*

Look at the picture. Read the word. Circle the -ed or -ing word that is spelled correctly.

1.	hop	hoping	hopeing	hopping
2.	bat	batted	bated	bateed
3.	skate	skating	skatting	skateing
4.	bike	bikked	biked	bikeed
5.	hug	huging	hugging	hugiing
6.	wave	waved	waveed	wavvd

Name ______________________

Adding *-ed, -ing*

Circle the word that fits in the sentence.

1. The cowboy ______________ a cow.

   ropped **roped**

2. A clown was ______________ a red flag.

   waveing **waving**

3. The bull ______________ running.

   stoped **stopped**

4. Kate ______________ Silver.

   peted **petted**

Name ______________________

Spelling Words Ending in *-ed*, *-ing*

Spelling Words

- mix
- mixed
- hop
- hopped
- hope
- hoping
- run
- running
- use
- used

Write the Spelling Words that end in -ing.

1. ______________ 2. ______________

Write the Spelling Words that end in -ed.

3. ______________ 4. ______________

5. ______________

Write the Spelling Words that are base words.

6. ______________ 7. ______________

8. ______________ 9. ______________

10. ______________

Name ____________________

What Is an Exclamation?

Draw a line under each exclamation.

1. The art show was great!

I saw many paintings.

2. Did you see the painting of the dog?

I liked that one the most!

3. Dee and Jan put the show together.

They did a good job!

4. I hope our class can see that show!

Don't you think so, too?

5. Kay saw the show yesterday.

She wants to see it again!

Name ______________________________

Showing Strong Feelings

Finish these sentences that tell your opinion about Vashti's teacher. Write one exclamation that shows a strong feeling.

Topic Sentence

I think Vashti's teacher is ______________________________

____

Detail Sentence

I think so because ______________________________

____

Detail Sentence

I also think so because ______________________________

____

Name ______________________________

Words with Long *e* Spelling Patterns *y, ie*

Circle the word that matches the picture. Write the word.

1.

bus bunny

____

2.

park party

____

3.

baby babies

____

4.

chief cheese

____

5.

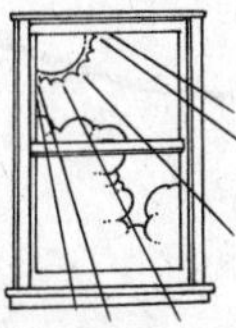

sunny seed

____

6.

when windy

____

Name ___

The Dot
Comprehension: Compare and Contrast

Compare and Contrast

Use the Venn diagram to compare and contrast writing and painting.

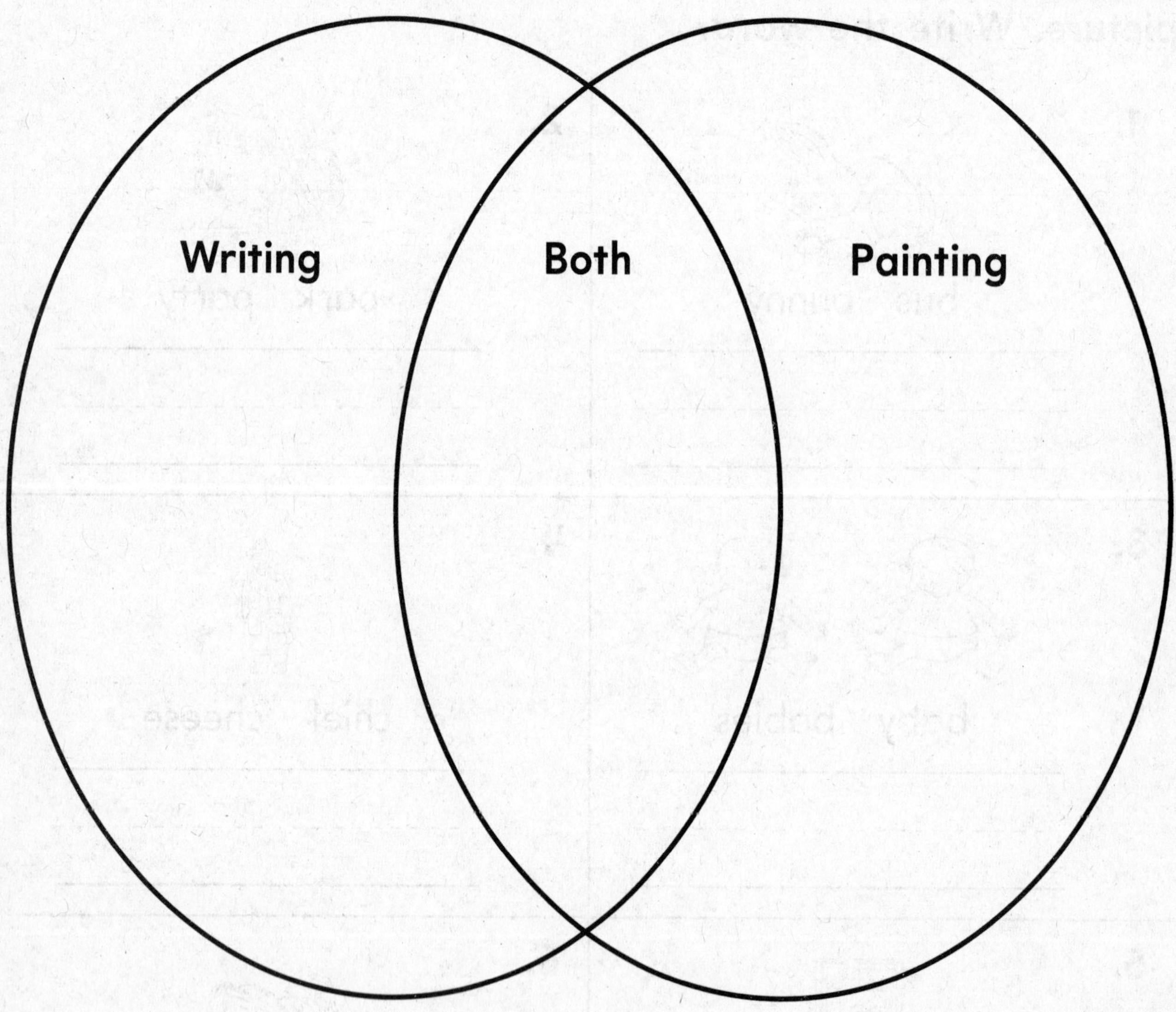

Name ______________________________

The Dot
Spelling: Words Ending in *cd*, *-ing*

Spelling Words Ending in *-ed*, *-ing*

Spelling Words

- mix
- mixed
- hop
- hopped
- hope
- hoping
- run
- running
- use
- used

Add -ed to each base word. Then write the new Spelling Word on the line.

1. mix ______________________

2. hop ______________________

3. use ______________________

Add -ing to each base word. Then write the new Spelling Word on the line.

4. hope ______________________

5. run ______________________

Name ______________________________

Writing Exclamations

Write each sentence as an exclamation. Begin and end the sentences correctly.

1. those paints are pretty

____

2. i love my new pencils

____

3. my painting got a prize

____

4. there is too much paper

____

5. we can't wait to draw

____

Name ______________________________

Planning My Sentences

 Write your opinion. Then write reasons that tell why.

My Opinion

First Reason

Second Reason

Name ______________________________

Words with Endings *-ed* and *-ing*

Write the Spelling Word to complete each sentence.

1. The bunny ____________ away.
(hop, hopped)

2. I ____________ I will win the race.
(hope, hoping)

3. He is ____________ very fast.
(run, running)

4. Kim ____________ all the glue in her art project.
(use, used)

5. I ____________ the eggs and the butter.
(mix, mixed)

Name ______________________________

Lesson 26
PRACTICE BOOK

The Dot
Grammar

Spiral Review

Circle the pronoun that can take the place of the underlined word or words.

1. Jack and Fred want to paint.

   We **They** **He**

2. Roy drew a picture of a puppy.

   It **He** **She**

3. The picture is very big.

   We **It** **He**

Write He, She, It, We, or They to take the place of the underlined word or words.

4. Jenny went to the art store. ______________

5. Rob and Liz were there. ______________

6. The store is a fun place. ______________

Name ______________________________

Grammar in Writing

An **exclamation** is a sentence that shows strong feeling. It ends with an exclamation point (!).

Example: Meg is an artist.

Revised: Meg is the best artist I know!

Revise each sentence. Make it an exclamation.

1. I like blue.

____

2. Mandy drew a picture.

____

3. Karl likes to paint.

____

4. Your pictures are nice.

____

Name ____________________

Words to Know

Circle the best answer to each question.

1. What word goes with **far**?	**near**	**high**
2. What word goes with **plot**?	**always**	**stories**
3. What word goes with **when**?	**different**	**once**
4. What word goes with **just right**?	**enough**	**near**
5. What word goes with **low**?	**high**	**happy**
6. What word goes with **sad**?	**once**	**happy**
7. What word goes with **never**?	**high**	**always**
8. What word goes with **same**?	**different**	**stories**

Name ______________________________

Adding *-er*, *-est* (change *y* to *i*)

Read the words. Circle the word that does not belong.

1. fancy	fancier	fanciest	find	
2. happy	happier	hand	happiest	
3. silly	sillier	silliest	still	
4. funny	far	funnier	funniest	
5. jolly	jollier	jolliest	joke	
6. messy	miss	messier	messiest	

Name ______________________________

What Can You Do?
Phonics: Adding *-er*, *-est* (change *y* to *i*)

Adding *-er*, *-est* (change *y* to *i*)

Circle the word that best completes the sentence.

1. My glue is ______ .

sticky **stickier**

2. That chick is the ______ of all.

fluffy **fluffiest**

3. This cupcake is ______ .

yummy **yummiest**

4. My hat is the ______ of all.

fancier **fanciest**

5. Her bird makes the ______ sounds.

sillier **silliest**

6. Luke tells ______ jokes.

funny **funnier**

Name ____________________

What Can You Do?
Spelling: Words Ending in *-er, -est*

Spelling Words Ending in *-er*, *-est*

Sort the words. Write the correct Spelling Words in each column.

Words with -er	Words with -est

Base words

Spelling Words

hard
harder
hardest
fast
faster
fastest
slow
slower
slowest
sooner

Name ______________________________

What Can You Do?
Grammar: Kinds of Sentences

Question or Exclamation?

Draw a line from each question to the question mark (?). Draw a line from each exclamation to the exclamation point (!).

1. I love to sing

2. Do you play drums

3. Sam wrote a great song

4. Can you cook

5. Mark makes the best snacks

6. May I have one

?
!

Name ______________________________

What Can You Do?
Writing: Write to Respond

Write Sentences with *Because*

Finish these sentences that tell your opinion about learning something new.

Topic Sentence

Learning to ____________ is ____________ .

hard easy

Detail Sentence

One reason is ______________________________
______________________________ .

Detail Sentence

Another reason is ______________________________
______________________________ .

Name ______________________________

Syllable *-le*

Circle the word that names the picture.

1.

bottle bubble

2.

handle candle

3.

paddle apple

4.

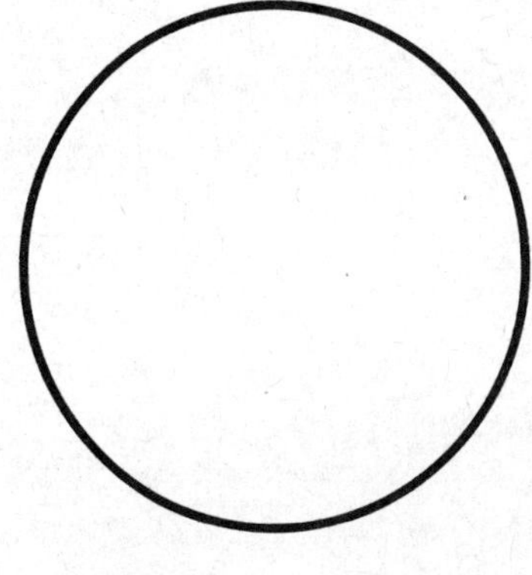

circle cattle

5.

bumble beetle

6.

poodle puzzle

Name ______________________________

Text and Graphic Features

Use the chart to tell about the features in **What Can You Do?** and their purposes.

Feature	Purpose

Name ____________________

What Can You Do?
Spelling: Words ending in *-er, -est*

Spelling Words Ending in *-er*, *-est*

Spelling Words

- hard
- harder
- hardest
- fast
- faster
- fastest
- slow
- slower
- slowest
- sooner

Add -er to each base word. Then write the new Spelling Word on the line.

1. hard ____________________

2. fast ____________________

3. slow ____________________

4. soon ____________________

Add -est to each base word. Then write the Spelling Word on the line.

5. hard ____________________

6. fast ____________________

7. slow ____________________

Name ______________________________

What Can You Do?
Grammar: Kinds of Sentences

Three Kinds of Sentences

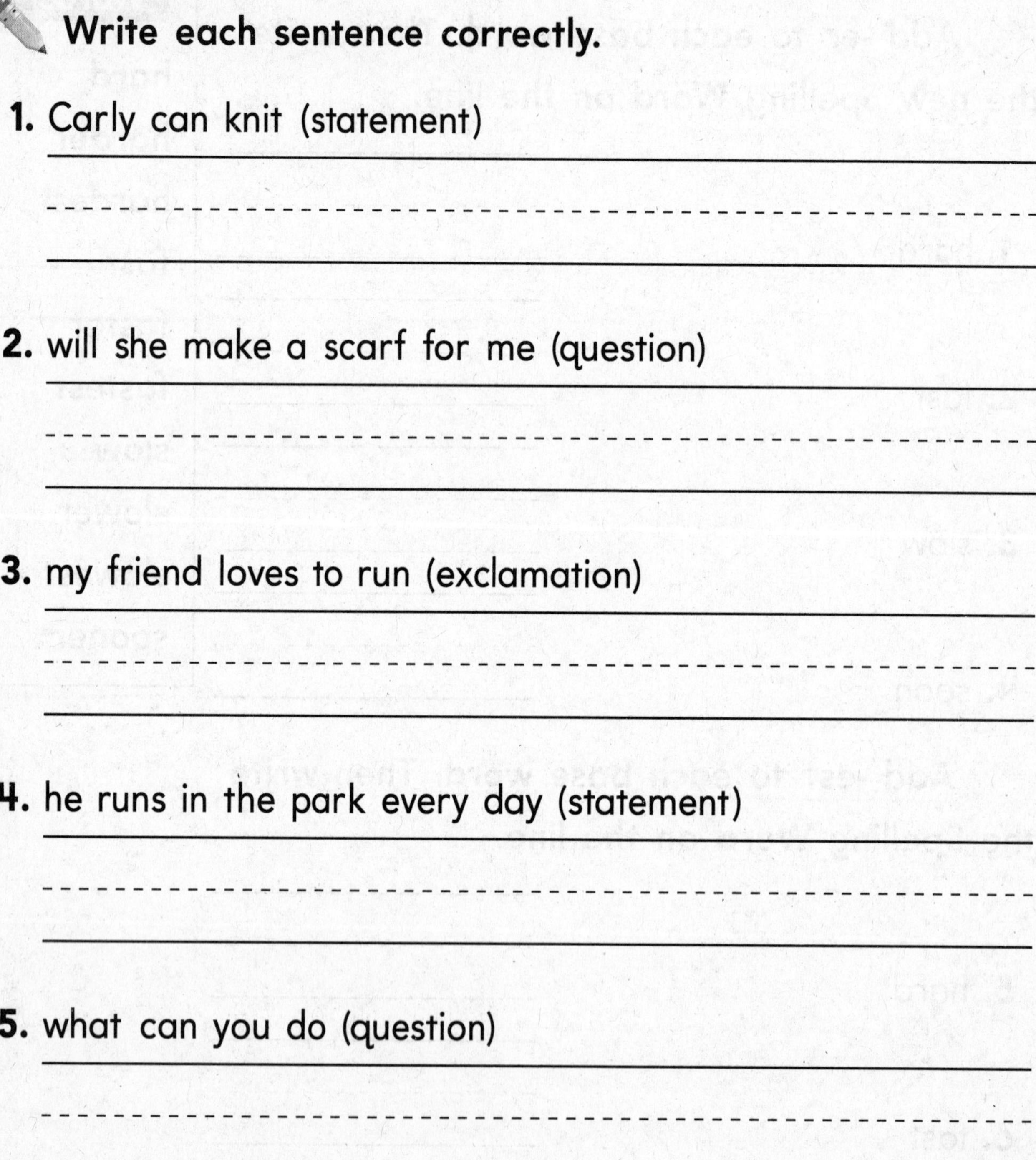

Write each sentence correctly.

1. Carly can knit (statement)

2. will she make a scarf for me (question)

3. my friend loves to run (exclamation)

4. he runs in the park every day (statement)

5. what can you do (question)

Name ____________________

What Can You Do?
Writing: Write to Respond

Planning My Sentences

Write your opinion. Then write reasons that tell why.

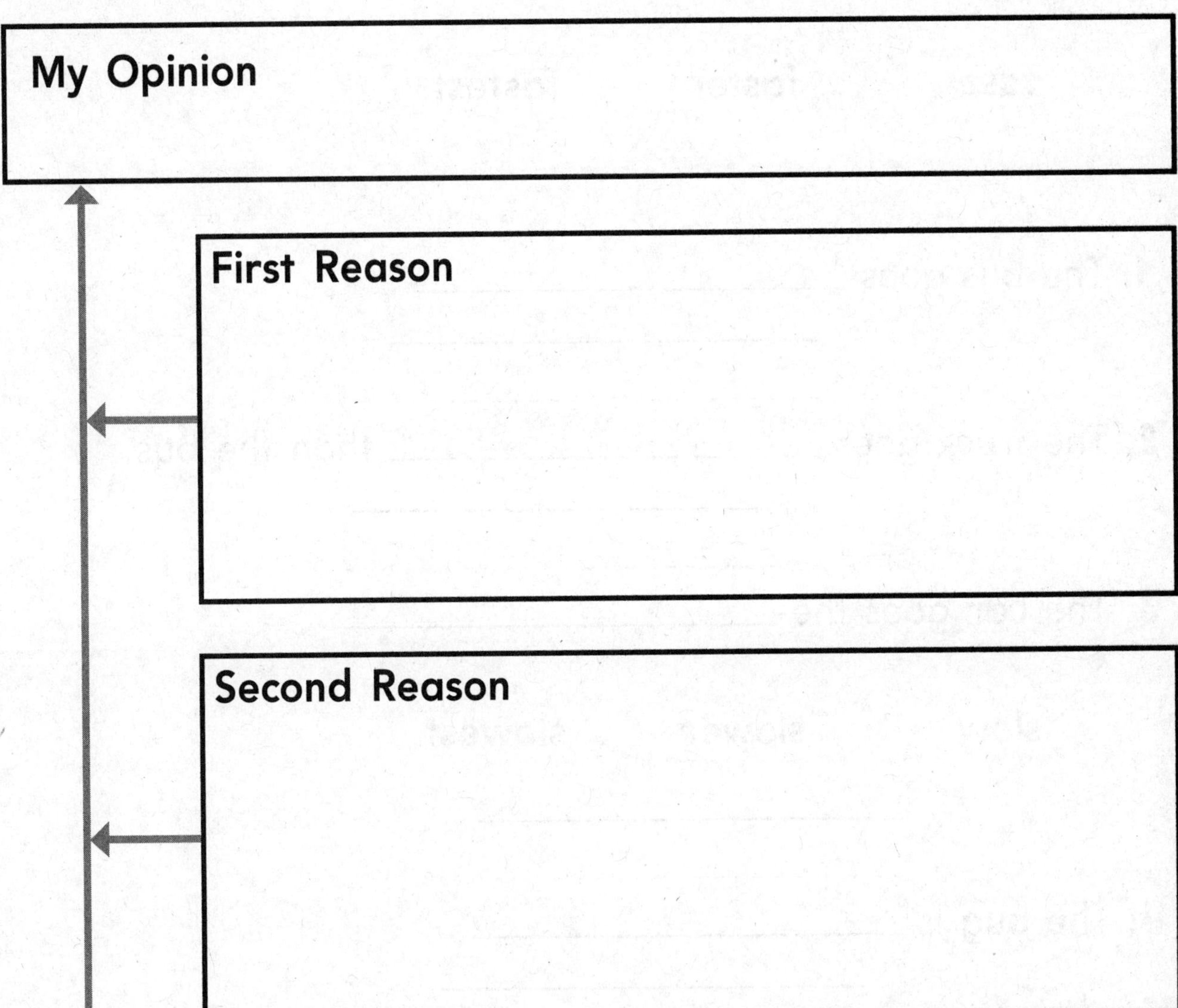

Name ______________________________

Words with Endings *-er* and *-est*

Write the Spelling Word that completes each sentence.

fast **faster** **fastest**

1. The bus goes ____________.

2. The truck goes ____________ than the bus.

3. The car goes the ____________.

slow **slower** **slowest**

4. The bug is ____________.

5. The worm is ____________ than the bug.

6. The turtle is the ____________ of all.

Name ______________________________

Spiral Review

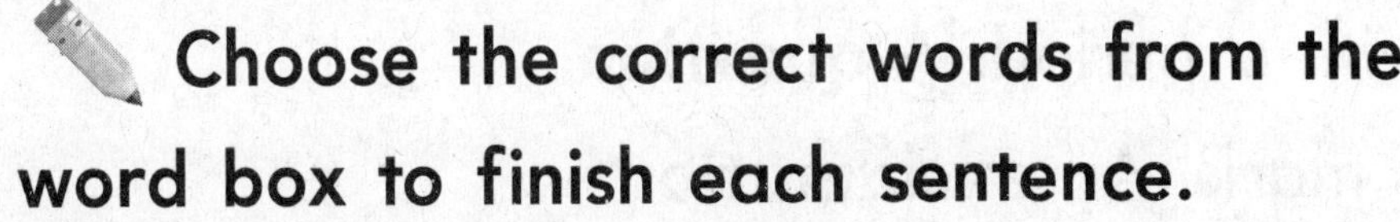

Choose the correct words from the word box to finish each sentence.

Mark	I	me

1. ____________ and ____________ act in a play.

I	Tammy	Me

2. ____________ and ____________ write stories.

Me	I	Ricky

3. ____________ and ____________ are friends.

I	Me	Sue

4. ____________ and ____________ like to slide.

Name ______________________________

Grammar in Writing

What Can You Do?
Grammar: Kinds of Sentences

A **statement** ends with a period. A **question** ends with a question mark. An **exclamation** ends with an exclamation point. All sentences begin with capital letters.

Revise each sentence. Change it to the kind shown in ( ).

Example: Glen can read. (question)
Can Glen read?

1. Is skating fun? (statement)

____

2. I like to ride my bike. (exclamation)

____

3. Chuck likes to act. (question)

____

4. Vicky writes the best stories! (statement)

____

Name ________________________________

Words to Know

Circle the correct word in each sentence.

1. The cat plays with a (ball, head) of yarn.

2. We all (cried, heard) the crash.

3. You (heard, should) try these grapes.

4. Jean is the (second, ball) girl in line.

5. "Let's go!" (cried, heard) Kenny.

6. My (large, head) hurts.

7. We are running (second, across) the field.

8. There is a (large, heard) bird in the tree.

Name ____________________

Lesson 28
PRACTICE BOOK

The Kite
Phonics: Long *i* Spelling Patterns *igh, y, ie*

Long *i* Spelling Patterns *igh, y, ie*

Look at the picture. Circle the word that names the picture.

1. 

spy line

2. 

pine pie

3. 

sky nine

4. 

high hive

5. 

think thigh

6. 

fine fly

Name ____________________

The Kite
Phonics: Long *i* Spelling Patterns *igh, y, ie*

Long *i* Spelling Patterns *igh*, *y*, *ie*

Write a word from the box to finish each sentence.

thigh	dry	try	tie	high

1. Sam hurt his ____________________ when he fell.

2. Dad's ____________________ has dots and stripes.

3. I will ____________________ to swim.

4. The bird will fly up ____________________.

5. The wet shirt will ____________________.

Name ______________________________

The Kite
Spelling: Words with Patterns *igh, y, ie*

Spelling Words with Patterns *igh*, *y*, *ie*

Spelling Words

my
try
sky
fly
by
dry
pie
cried
night
light

Write the Spelling Words with the igh pattern.

1. ____________ 2. ____________

Write the Spelling Words with the ie pattern.

3. ____________ 4. ____________

Write the Spelling Words with the y spelling.

5. ____________ 6. ____________

7. ____________ 8. ____________

9. ____________ 10. ____________

Name ________________________________

Adjectives for Taste and Smell

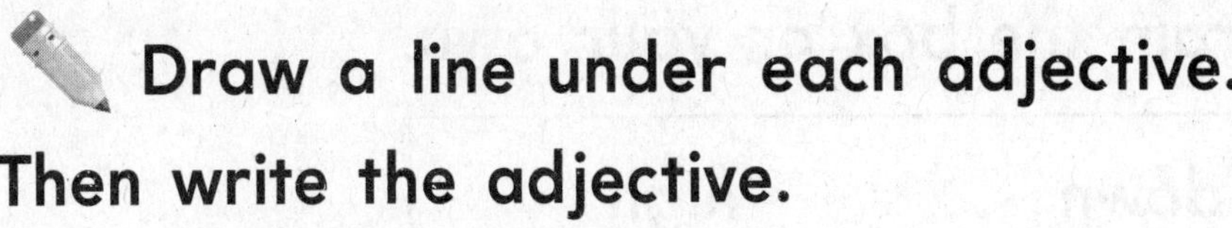

Draw a line under each adjective. Then write the adjective.

1. I smell the sweet roses.

____

2. We taste the bitter lemon.

____

3. Does the milk smell sour?

____

4. The chips taste spicy.

____

5. The toast smells burnt.

____

Name ______________________________

Using Different Words

Change a repeated word to an exact word. Use a word from the box or your own.

bright	down	high
flew	funny	blue
mean	ran	sunny

Toad went fast, and the kite went up.

Toad ______________ fast, and the kite went up.

The little birds laughed at Toad's little kite.

The little birds laughed at Toad's ______________ kite.

The pretty kite danced in the pretty sky.

The pretty kite danced in the ______________ sky.

Name ______________________________

Adding *-ed*, *-ing*, *-er*, *-est*, *-es*

Write the word that best completes each sentence. Use words from the box.

smaller	jumped	riding	highest	foxes

1. Those trees are the ______________ of all.

2. That bird is ______________ than this one.

3. Who is ______________ a red bike?

4. A frog ______________ into the pond.

5. Five ______________ ran to the woods.

Name ______________________________

Story Structure

Use the Story Map to tell about the characters, setting, and plot of The Kite.

Characters	**Setting**
Plot	
Beginning	
Middle	
End	

Name ______________________________

Spelling Words with Patterns *igh*, *y*, *ie*

Write each group of Spelling Words in ABC order.

my try sky fly by	dry pie cried night light
________________	________________
________________	________________
________________	________________
________________	________________
________________	________________

Spelling Words

my
try
sky
fly
by
dry
pie
cried
night
light

Name ______________________________

Adjectives for Sound and Texture

 **Draw a line under each adjective. Then write the adjective.**

1. We sail on the smooth lake.

____

2. I hear the loud cry of a seagull.

____

3. The sun feels warm.

____

4. The frog sings with a soft voice.

____

5. Do not step on those sharp rocks.

____

Name ______

Planning My Sentences

 **Write your opinion. Then write reasons that tell why.**

My Opinion

First Reason

Second Reason

Name ______________________________

Spelling Words with *igh*, *y*, *ie*

Write the correct word to complete each sentence.

1. Please turn on the ______________.
(cried, light, pie)

2. Have you seen ______________ book?
(my, try, night)

3. The baby ______________ in her crib.
(fly, dry, cried)

4. Make sure to ______________ the dishes.
(dry, my, light)

5. We went to a great play last ______________.
(light, night, fly)

Name ______________________________

Spiral Review

Write the correct pronoun to finish each sentence.

1. Is the yellow kite ______________?

   your **yours**

2. That is ______________ kite.

   her **hers**

3. Rex put away ______________ kite.

   he **his**

4. Would you like to play at ______________ house?

   my **mine**

5. We can fly the kite that is ______________.

   my **mine**

Name ______________________________

Grammar in Writing

Some adjectives describe nouns by telling about **taste**, **smell**, **sound**, or **feel**.

Example: I feel the ^cool breeze.

Revise each sentence. Use the proofreading mark to add an adjective.

sweet	fresh	happy	soft

1. Mr. Bee shares some honey.

2. The frog gave a croak.

3. We sit on the grass.

4. We enjoy the air.

Proofreading Mark	
^	add

Name ____________________

Words to Know

Circle the correct word to complete each sentence.

1. Raking the yard is a good (any, idea).

2. The (leaves, happened) are a pretty red.

3. Summer is (gone, any), and fall is here.

4. Bill is (behind, almost) the tree.

5. Sal waves (hello, gone) to Bess.

6. What (behind, happened) when Bill jumped in the leaves?

7. (Idea, Any) pal can help us rake.

8. We are (leaves, almost) done raking.

Name ______________________________

A Boat Disappears
Phonics: Words with Suffixes *-ful*, *-ly*, *-y*

Suffixes *-ful*, *-ly*, *-y*

 **Write a suffix from the box to finish the word.**

ful	ly	y

1. sad ________

2. bump ________

3. dust ________

4. help ________

5. slow ________

6. safe ________

Name ______________________

A Boat Disappears
Phonics: Words with Suffixes *-ful, ly, y*

Suffixes *-ful*, *-ly*, *-y*

Choose a word from the box. Choose a suffix to make a new word. Write the new word below the suffix.

spoon	snow	sad	trick	
joy	quick	peace	dirt	glad

y	ly	ful

Name ______________________

Spelling Words with the Suffixes *-ly, -y, -ful*

Spelling Words

- sad
- sadly
- slow
- slowly
- dust
- dusty
- trick
- tricky
- help
- helpful

Write the Spelling Words with -ly.

1. ______________ 2. ______________

Write the Spelling Words with -y.

3. ______________ 4. ______________

Write the Spelling Word with -ful.

5. ______________

Write the Spelling Words that are base words.

6. ______________ 7. ______________

8. ______________ 9. ______________

10. ______________

Name ______________________________

Adverbs for How and Where

Circle the adverb in each sentence. Write it on the line.

1. The inspector went upstairs. ____________

2. McBugg followed him closely. ____________

3. Skeet is here. ____________

4. He watched the bug carefully. ____________

Complete each sentence. Write an adverb that tells how or where.

5. The leaf floated ____________ down the stream.

6. Skeet stores his new boat ____________ .

Name ___________________________

Giving Examples

Look at the drawing in your book of Inspector Hopper's office. Write your opinion about the office.

I think Inspector Hopper's office is ______________.

Write one reason to explain your opinion.

One reason is ___________________________

Write two examples to explain your reason.

1. ___________________________

2. ___________________________

Name ______________________

Long Vowel Spelling Patterns *a, e, i, o, u*

Circle the two words in each row that rhyme. Then write the letter that spells the long vowel sound.

1. table hi fable me ______

2. hi she he go ______

3. kind no flu mind ______

4. flu Stu so be ______

5. we hold wind told ______

Name ______________________________

Cause and Effect

Use the chart to write about what happened in A Boat Disappears and why it happened.

What Happened?	Why Did It Happen?

Name ______________________________

Spelling Words with the Suffixes *-ly, -y, -ful*

A Boat Disappears
Spelling: Words with *-ly, -y, -ful*

Spelling Words

sad
sadly
slow
slowly
dust
dusty
trick
tricky
help
helpful

Add -ly to each base word. Then write the new Spelling Word on the line.

1. sad ______________________
2. slow ______________________

Add -y to each base word. Then write the new Spelling Word on the line.

3. dust ______________________
4. trick ______________________

Add -ful to the base word. Then write the new Spelling Word on the line.

5. help ______________________

Name ______________________________

Adverbs for When and How Much

Circle the adverb in each sentence. Write it on the line.

1. The water is too high to cross. ____________

2. Skeet arrived late to the picnic. ____________

3. He was very happy to see his friends. ____________

4. They will have a boat race soon. ____________

Complete each sentence. Write an adverb that tells when or how much.

5. We will have a picnic ____________.

6. The bucket was ____________ full.

Name ______________________

Words with the Suffixes *-ly, -y, -ful*

Write the correct word from the box to complete each sentence.

trick
tricky

1. I did a card ____________.

trick
tricky

2. It was ____________ to find the way to the park.

help
helpful

3. I like to ____________ wash the car.

4. When I wash the car, I am very ____________.

help
helpful

sad
sadly

5. I was ____________ to hear my mom call me home.

sad
sadly

6. I ____________ walked home.

Name ______________________

Spiral Review

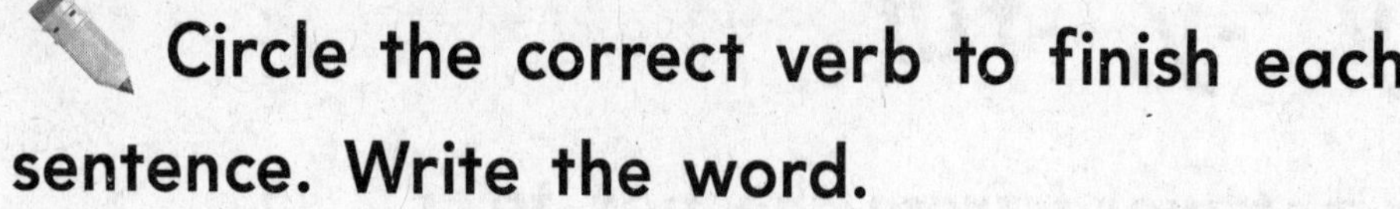

Circle the correct verb to finish each sentence. Write the word.

1. I ______________ with my friends.

   am   is

2. We ______________ by the lake.

   sit   sits

2. It ______________ a sunny day.

   is   am

3. We ______________ hungry.

   is   are

5. He ______________ snacks.

   bring   brings

Name ____________________

A Boat Disappears
Writing: Write to Respond

Planning My Opinion Paragraph

Write your opinion. Then write reasons and examples.

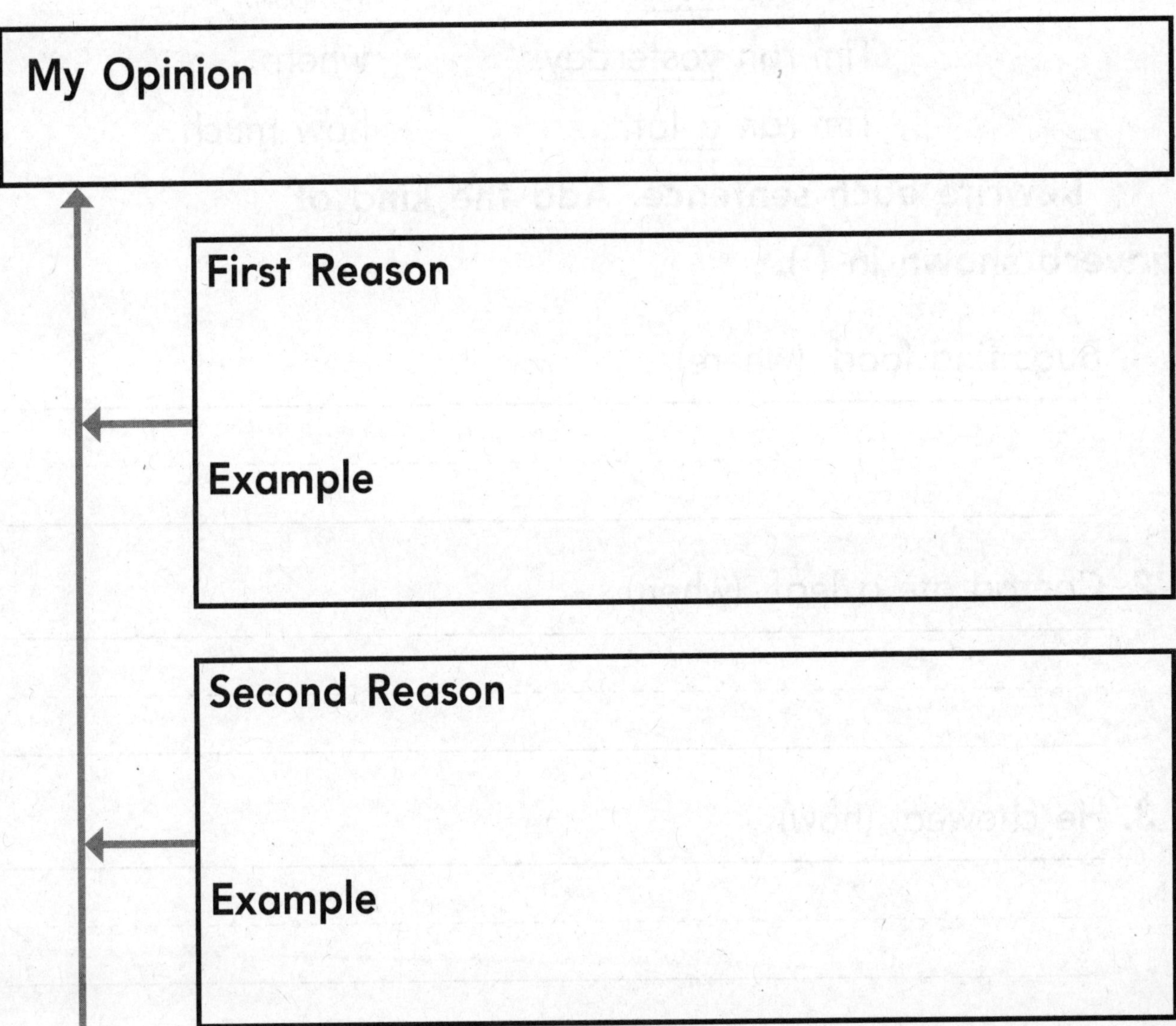

Name ____________________

Grammar in Writing

Adverbs can tell **how**, **where**, **when**, or **how much**.

Examples:	Tim ran <u>quickly</u>.	how
	Tim ran <u>here</u>.	where
	Tim ran <u>yesterday</u>.	when
	Tim ran <u>a lot</u>.	how much

Rewrite each sentence. Add the kind of adverb shown in ( ).

1. Bugs find food. (where)

____

2. Conrad ate a leaf. (when)

____

3. He chewed. (how)

____

4. He ate. (how much)

____

Name ______________________________

Words to Know

 Circle the best answer to each clue.

1. This means **all people.**	everyone	field
2. This means **liked a lot.**	most	loved
3. These are children and adults.	sorry	people
4. **Sisters** is its opposite.	brothers	loved
5. This is a place to play soccer.	most	field
6. This means **almost all.**	people	most
7. This means **a certain number.**	field	only
8. This is a **kind of feeling.**	sorry	everyone

Name ____________________

Syllable Pattern CV

Read each word. Draw a line to divide the CV word into two syllables.

1.

music might

2.

baby bone

3.

lace lady

4.

part pilot

5.

robber robot

6.

motel miss

Name ____________________

Syllable Pattern CV

In each sentence, circle the CV word that has two syllables.

1. It is a bright, shiny day!
2. There is a huge hotel by the lake.
3. Big boats sail in the wavy tide.
4. I hope you decide to come see me.
5. We could take a slow, lazy ride on a boat.

Name ______________________________

Spelling Words with CV Syllables

Write the Spelling Words with the long e sound in the first syllable.

1. ______________ 2. ______________

3. ______________ 4. ______________

Write the Spelling Words with the long a sound in the first syllable.

5. ______________ 6. ______________

7. ______________

Write the Spelling Words with these long vowel sounds in the first syllable.

8. long **i** ______________ 9. long **o** ______________

10. long **u** ______________

Spelling Words

- even
- open
- begin
- baby
- tiger
- music
- paper
- zero
- table
- below

Name ______________________________

Adjectives with *er* and *est*

Circle the correct adjective to finish each sentence. Write the adjective.

1. Tim is ____________ than Max.

   taller **tallest**

2. Fred is the ____________ of them all.

   taller **tallest**

3. Cathy is ____________ than Cam.

   older **oldest**

4. Adam is the ____________ player of all.

   smaller **smallest**

Name ______________________________

Writing a Closing Sentence

Do you think Mia should have quit? Write your own words that explain your opinion. Listen to the words in the Word Bank. Read along. Be sure your last sentence retells your opinion.

Word Bank

agree **disagree** **decision** **reason** **example**

____

I ______________________________ with Mia's decision to ______________________________

quit. One reason is ______________________________.

____

For example, ______________________________.

____

Another reason is ______________________________.

____

I think ______________________________.

Name ____________________

Winners Never Quit!
Phonics: Words with Prefixes *un-*, *re-*

Prefixes *un-*, *re-*

Read each word. Circle the word in each box that matches the picture.

1.

untie tried

2.

read repaint

3.

setting remove

4.

bedding unbraid

5.

untidy neat

6.

unzip unbutton

Name ______________________________

Understanding Characters

Use the chart to tell what Mia thinks, what she says, and what she does in **Winners Never Quit!**

Thinks	Says	Does

Name ______________________

Spelling Words with Syllables CV

Write the Spelling Word that fits each clue.

1. Opposite of **closed** ______________
2. A very young person ______________
3. Something to listen to ______________
4. Opposite of **end** ______________
5. Opposite of **above** ______________
6. An animal ______________

Spelling Words

- even
- open
- begin
- baby
- tiger
- music
- paper
- zero
- table
- below

Name ______________________________

Using the Right Adjective

Write adjectives from the Word Banks to finish the sentences.

Word Bank

green **greener** **greenest**

1. Our yard is ____________ .

2. Your yard is ____________ than ours.

3. His yard is the ____________ of all.

Word Bank

long **longer** **longest**

4. We played a ____________ game today.

5. The game yesterday was ____________ than the game today.

Name ______________________________

Spelling Words with Syllable Pattern CV

Write the correct word to complete each sentence.

1. Ken saw a ____________ at the zoo.
(below, tiger)

2. Please sit and ____________ your test.
(even, begin)

3. What kind of ____________ do you like?
(below, music)

4. I used red ____________ to make the card.
(paper, zero)

5. The food is on the ____________.
(open, table)

Name ______________________________

Spiral Review

Choose contractions from the box for the underlined words. Write the contractions.

Word Bank

He's
can't
She's
isn't

1. She is a tennis player.

____

2. I cannot wait to play with her.

____

3. It is not hard to play.

____

4. He is learning now!

____

Name ____________________

Grammar in Writing

- Add **er** to adjectives to compare two.
- Add **est** to compare more than two.

Example: Today is warm.

Today is the warmest day of the summer.

Revise each sentence. Use an adjective that compares. Add other words, too.

1. Beth is a fast runner.

____

2. Tad is tall.

____

3. Our team is stronger.

____

4. Today was cold.

____